The Father's Love

An Encounter with God the Father

Bruce Lindley

Foreword by Ché Ahn

The Father's Love
by R. Bruce Lindley

Copyright © 2016 Bruce Lindley
Published by
Australian Apostolic Restore Community (A.A.R.C.)
PO Box 4393, Helensvale B.C. QLD 4212, Australia

This book or parts thereof may not be reproduced in any form, stored in a retrieval system, or transmitted in any form by any means – electronic, mechanical, photocopy, recording or otherwise – without prior written permission of the publisher, except as provided by Australian copyright law.

Unless otherwise noted, quotations are taken from the HOLY BIBLE, NEW INTERNATIONAL VERSION. Copyright © 2011 by Zondervan. Used by permission of Zondervan. All rights reserved.

Scripture quotations marked (NASB) taken from the NEW AMERICAN STANDARD BIBLE®, Copyright ©1960, 1962, 1963, 1968, 1971, 1972, 1973, 1975, 1977, 1995 by The Lockman Foundation. Used by permission.

Scripture quotations marked (NLT) taken from Holy Bible. New Living Translation copyright© 1996, 2004, 2007, 2013 by Tyndale House Foundation. Used by permission of Tyndale House Publishers Inc., Carol Stream, Illinois 60188. All rights reserved.

Scripture quotations marked (NKJV) taken from the New King James Version®. Copyright © 1982 by Thomas Nelson. Used by permission. All rights reserved.

ISBN: 978-0-9942402-1-7

Printed in Australia

Dedication

The Father's Love is dedicated to my Heavenly Father who overwhelmed me with HIS love to the point that I was adopted as His son and transformed for eternity.

It is also dedicated to my precious wife Cheryl whose love inspires and challenges me to new depths of encountering God the Father and to my wonderful children and spiritual children for whom I love. You have helped me to love in the way God the Father always intended us to love.

Acknowledgements

This book wouldn't have been possible without the support and help of my amazing Cheryl Lindley – a true reflection of the Father's love. And to our wonderful Apostolic Restore Community (ARC International) family – Thank you for living the kingdom of God with us.

Special thanks to Carol Martinez for her wonderful editing skills.

Contents

Foreword - Ché Ahn 7

Introduction – The Father's Love 11

1. Why We Need the Father's love 17
2. Becoming Sons and Daughters 31
3. Intimacy with the Father 37
4. Because of His Lavish Love 59
5. Your Identity as His Child 71
6. Living as a Child of the Father 85
7. Your Inheritance as Daddy's child 91
8. The Real You Is Being Revealed 97
9. Soaring in Your Sonship on Purpose 107
10. Your Sonship Position 123
11. Your Posture as a Son of God 131

Conclusion 141

Endnotes 145

Australian Apostolic Resource Community (A.A.R.C.) 147

Contact and Resource Details 148

Foreword

by Ché Ahn

Those who study human development will tell you that the three basic needs that every person has are shelter, food and clothing. However, those are merely needs for survival that have no bearing on our success and fulfillment as individuals. I would say that studies which have taken place all over the world on development of infants point us to an unequivocal truth: our greatest need is that of love – to be loved and to love. In fact, there are a number of scientific studies which reveal reports that infants who are lacking touch and emotional engagement suffer from hormonal imbalances, health issues, social, emotional, and behavioral problems.

What is my point? We are living in a day and age in which a generation of 'fatherless' baby boomers have passed on a sense of fatherlessness to the next generations – and we are seeing the effects of unseen numbers of people struggling with depression, anxiety, hormonal imbalance, and social, emotional and behavioral dysfunction on a global scale. And still the 'antidote', as Bruce so aptly names it, is the Father's love. This is a simple and profound reality.

There is no better timing for this moving book, *The Father's Love*, written by pastor, apostle, and longtime friend Bruce Lindley.

The Apostle Paul, in Ephesians 3:17-19, prays that,

'Christ may dwell in your hearts through faith; that you, being rooted and grounded in love, may be able to comprehend with all the saints what is the width and length and depth and height—to know the love of Christ which passes knowledge; that you may be filled with all the fullness of God. (NKJV)

The love Jesus has for us is the love the Father has for us. Most people spend their lives trying to meet their legitimate need for this incalculable love illegitimately – never knowing why their need isn't met. It is only in letting the Father love us and knowing the love that He has for us that we will be fulfilled and radically transformed. It is the true love of our true Father – the truest Father – the true Vine and the true Vinedresser (John 15) – that melts the hardest of hearts.

Bruce fearlessly addresses the heart of the matter – healing our orphan hearts and eradicating the stronghold of the orphan spirit. The love of the Father heals the Orphan Heart – the heart that wages war against the other; the heart that says that there is 'never enough'; the heart that never dares to dream; the heart that rages against sound judgment and authority; the heart that cries for attention but fears it at the same time; the heart that desperately needs to feel significant but never does. For it is the orphan who hides, because he/she never feels accepted. He/she craves intimacy, but is terrified by it all the same. But God. The Father wants to heal all of this and has done it through Jesus, we must only accept it.

The Father's heart covers us, affirms us and undoes any cause for shame and hiding. He brings us out before the crowds and shouts, 'here is My son and daughter, in whom I am pleased.' The Father's heart gives us our significance, a significance that cannot be understood outside of knowing that we were so significant that the Father gave and sacrificed Jesus for us. The Father's love pursues intimacy with us, knowing us better than we know ourselves, and gives us our dreams and the favor and grace needed to see them come to pass.

The love of God is powerful enough to break the stronghold on generations who, Bruce so truly stated, have pulled away from their Father God. His love is enough to bring them back home – just as in the parable of the Prodigal Son.

Any remaining scales of the orphan spirit that have lingered in your life will fall off upon the reading of *The Father's Love*, by Bruce Lindley, as the delight of the Father is so emphatically revealed in its pages, and our identity as sons and daughters of God will go from a religious knowledge to a tangible experience that will shake and shift us, no matter how long we have been walking with the Lord.

Through activation decrees and questions, Bruce intentionally moves us from passive readers to active participants in our relationship with the Father. We transition from waiting for God to do something to running into the arms of the One Who loves us best and loves us first. We are encouraged to make room for Him.

May the Father's love wash over you as you read these pages and may you receive the keys to identity, inheritance, destiny, purpose and authority that a radical encounter with the love of God can give you.

Dr. Ché Ahn
President and Founder
Harvest International Ministry

Introduction

THE FATHER'S LOVE

The greatest human need we have is love! We were never meant to live alone. As my wife Cheryl has always said, 'God sets everyone in families.'

She is right. God is a good Father and He wants us to experience His Father's love.

His intent was that we also experience love through family. God created us with the need for our father and mother's love, regardless of our upbringing. The greatest gift a child can have is to know that they are loved by their mother and father and experience that love DAILY.

Even though many of our fathers and mothers did a less than perfect job at this, their true role in the purest sense is to teach us what love is supposed to look like. But many parents fall short of that which is why people often struggle to experience the love of God the Father.

As we grow up we begin to look to others for love.

Many people spend their entire lives searching for that perfect love – looking for Miss or Mister Right. When they don't find him or her, they shop around changing partners, sometimes repetitively, until they finally settle for less. But often they live a dissatisfied existence.

Just recently we were doing some renovation in our home and a carpenter came to install some doors for us. He was constantly on the phone and seemed very distracted. I asked him if anything was wrong and he told me that he was in the middle of a divorce. He went on to explain that a few months earlier his wife had advised him, 'I'm no longer in love with you.' He was clearly upset, angry, and heartbroken. He told me that his wife had found somebody else but then he went on to tell me that he was also looking for that other special someone.

When I was a pastor, I often gave premarital counseling to couples before they got married. One of the things that I would always say is that we spell 'love' wrongly. I would say, 'Love is spelt with a C'. That always got their attention. I would go on to explain that it is spelt with the C of Commitment. To love selflessly you need to have commitment deep in your soul. When you first fall in love, emotions carry you. If that is all you have, then when the emotions begin to fade you will think you are no longer in love. But true love is not just an emotion. True love is a covenant of commitment to love no matter what!

I have learnt that emotions in love can be like the tide in the ocean. At times the tide goes out, but it is an unwritten law of nature that the tide always comes in again. So if you have commitment deep in your soul, the tide of emotion in love will always come back in again.

We also encourage all married couples and families to pray together each day. My wife also says, 'It's hard to continue to be upset at someone when you hear their heart of love toward God'. Praying together causes forgiveness and reconciliation to flow freely. This type of love works. Why? Because it is supernatural.

However, the bottom line is that you need God the Father's love to be married to an imperfect person. The only true way to love another and also feel 'fully loved' is to have an intimate relationship with the source of all love – God the Father.

The 'apostle of love' John 'the beloved' taught this truth to everyone who would listen.

He decreed in 1 John 4:16:

'God is love. Whoever lives in love lives in God, and God in them.'

The truth is that the only person who can truly fill your love vacuum is not a human being! It is God the Father Himself whom you are looking for. If you don't fill your love vacuum with the Father's love you will never be satisfied and will always try to fill it with other things.

My prayer is that you would not only know that with your mind, but you would experience the love of God the Father and live in His love in a way you have never experienced before.

It Is God the Father's Love that You Are Looking For

While most Christians know intellectually that God loves them, most of us never know just how much love He has ALREADY given us!

I remember as a teenager as one of three growing boys in our family, how hungry we would always be. It seemed no matter how much food our mother served us for dinner, we would always be looking for more at the end. Without fail my mother would say, 'I'm not hungry; have mine'. It was only when I became a parent feeding growing children that I realized that my mum was hungry, but willingly sacrificed her food in love for us.

When our first daughter Rebecca was born, she struggled with colic and would cry in pain non-stop for hours and hours. One night in the very early hours of the morning as I was walking the floor trying to comfort her and get her back to sleep, I realized that my mother had done that exact same thing for me. I was overwhelmed. At other times I would look at my children asleep and my heart would ache with love for them. The most amazing thing is that God loves us even more!

The love of a parent does not even compare with the love that the Father has for us. In fact, we are told that there is no measure to the love that He has for us. It is limitless. And we need to begin to see and understand how great this love is.

1 John 3:1 says,

'SEE what great love the Father has lavished on us, that we should be called children of God! And that is what we are!' (Upper case added.)

We have to see with the Father's Eyes. If we don't see with the Father's eyes we won't comprehend how great His love is for us.

The way to do this is that we need to see through the 'spirit of adoption'. Something amazing happens when you experience the spirit of adoption. Your life is transformed by the Father's love.

When we see Him as He truly is – then we will truly know our Father's love. This great love is not ordinary love or human conditional love. It is not emotion that wears off and doesn't last or satisfy.

It is unconditional love that has no limit to its giving, to its depth, or to its dimension.

There is no end to His Love! This is not a romantic fantasy love that you see in movies.

No, Papa God's love truly satisfies and completes you and fulfils the desire in your heart to be loved!

His great love for you is limitless. My earnest prayer for you is that you will encounter more of the Father's love for yourself as you read this book.

We have included practical activations and decrees throughout this book so you actually have an encounter with the Father's love. If you take the time to encounter Him you will never be the same.

Chapter 1

WHY WE NEED THE FATHER'S LOVE

A father's love is so important. However, society no longer sees it as a priority. We are living more and more in a 'fatherless era'.

A reality television series called 'The World's Strictest Parents' began in Australia a few years ago. I found it hard to watch but decided I must, as I knew it offered insight into the current fatherless heart in our culture.

The basis of the show was about badly behaving rebellious teenagers who were not listening to father or mother figures in their lives. They typically were from a family where there were no or very few boundaries. As part of the show they were suddenly uprooted and flown overseas and placed in a family with very strict boundaries. As expected, they instantly clashed as they had no respect for anybody in authority.

One episode was about a rebellious Australian teenager who was taken to live in the South in the United States. He lied and disobeyed continuously. Every time he disobeyed the host father, the teenager discovered that there were consequences. Due to repeated disobedience he was eventually required to volunteer in the kitchen of a homeless shelter.

One day he broke the rules in the shelter and actually caused a major problem. The host father lovingly but clearly showed him that his actions were actually life threatening to the residents of the shelter. It really sobered the teenage boy when he realized the potential consequences of his behavior. The next day he publically apologized to the whole shelter.

He had encountered a Father's love that would not move.

This was a turning point for him. He had discovered the power of loving boundaries. For ten days he had challenged every boundary. Then on the last day something shifted in the teenager. His eyes were opened and he apologised and listened to what the father was saying.

The last scene of the program was when they were saying goodbye to each other before the teenager returned back to his own home. The guest father said to this wayward boy, 'It would be an honor for me to have you as my son.' Up to this point this boy lived and behaved as one who was fatherless but when he had an encounter with a true father, something was triggered inside him. He put his head on the guest father's shoulder and cried and hugged him for a long time.

The program then 'fast forwards' to months later after the teenager had returned home to Australia. This boy had changed completely. He was still emailing his new 'father figure' at least once or twice a week and had changed his attitude and behavior completely toward his own parents and those around him.

This is what the love of a true father does. It transforms even the hardest heart.

We Are In a New Era

It is important to reflect on this because we are in the era of God turning the heart of the fathers to the children and the children to the fathers.

We recently received a prophecy that God was speaking to us from Malachi 4:5-6:

'I will turn the heart of the fathers to the children and the heart of the children to their fathers so I will not come and strike the land with a curse'.

This is the time for us all to experience God as our Father in a whole new way. It is a time of great change in the body of Christ. God is decreeing through Isaiah 43:19:

'See, I am doing a new thing. Now it springs up'.

It is now! God is doing new things *for* us and *in* us.

We are seeing so many changes happening in nations around the world. Never before have we seen so much change of political leaders, presidents being overthrown, economies collapsing and refugees flooding to other nations. We are in an era of great change!

This has been highlighted in Australian politics. We have had seven different prime ministers in nine years. Depending on your political persuasion some would say that some of these changes were necessary. At least one of the changes involved a restoration of an injustice where the current prime minister was replaced in a leadership challenge by a previous prime minister who had been betrayed by his own political party.

A very significant sequel took place the next day after this change. The former prime minister was seated in the back of the parliament listening to an independent member speak about this sudden transition of leadership. He was not from her political party but he had helped her to form a minority government at the previous election.

In the course of his speech he turned to her and said something very loving and kind. He said, *'Your father would be proud of you the way you conducted yourself.'* In response, this battle-hardened, tough politician began to cry in the middle of our House of Representatives. When I saw this, it struck me how much our leaders also lack fathering.

Once you become aware of the orphan heart, you see it everywhere. Politicians being defensive trying to protect their leadership; leaders feeling threatened by a younger leader emerging quickly.

Why are fathers so important? There is something inherent in human nature that cries out for a family: the need for a mother who nurtures and the need for a father who gives security, strength, value and whole love to their children.

Many fathers did not have good father role models in their own life; whether they had an actual biological father or not, in many senses they were raised as orphans. Then, sadly, out of their lack of wholeness , they in turn also reproduce orphans … And the cycle goes on.

We have a generation of young people who aren't being fathered. Instead, they are being mentored and molded by what they are listening to and seeing on social media; Twitter, Facebook, Netflix and similar.

Typically, their fathers, those known as 'baby boomers' (those born post World War II in the late 1940s, 1950s, 1960s and even 1970s) were not fathered either. Why? Fatherlessness had been passed down from generation to generation. The orphan origin of most nations (especially Australia) and traumatic experiences in wars contributed to this in great measure. Fathers were so broken they were shut down and could not show any emotion. We knew our fathers loved us but we would never hear them say it. They were stuck!

As a teenager, we would drive past an orphanage on our way to school. As I looked into the vacant grounds and saw the sterile buildings, I found it to be a very intimidating place. I was glad I had a family, a mother and father and that I didn't have to live in an institution. Years later I had the opportunity to actually visit that orphanage. I met young people who longed to be loved. Many of them were acting badly. Even then I realised they were seeking attention because of their hunger for love.

But they were not the only ones who longed to be loved. We had an entire generation growing up longing for love. The Beatles summed it up when they sang, *All you need is love.* The truth is that the youth of our nations were ailing with an orphan heart – a heart looking for love, acceptance and encouragement from fathers and father figures who believed in them. Who would tell them that they could make it? That they were awesome? Sadly, this sort of encouragement is still very lacking in all cultures.

I grew up with parents who both experienced a World War firsthand. While I knew they loved me, they rarely showed any affection. I discovered that this was pretty typical of that generation. They didn't know any better because it was the way their parents had treated them. It seemed that the orphan spirit was deep in the heart of our culture. Not only a lack of affection but also a lack of intimacy with God, fathers, spouses, and children. I was often told by my parents and other adults that 'children should be seen and not heard'. I remember as a young person trying to understand what that phrase really meant. In fact it summed up an orphan heart attitude that had been passed from one generation of parents to the next. It was an attitude of intolerance, rejection and a lack of outward affection and intimacy.

When we are truly intimate with God the Father we run to Him not away from Him. In Australia, men who returned from both the First and Second World Wars ran away from God. This was reflected in the decline in attendance at church by these men. It seemed they blamed God for the horrors of war rather than recognising the war was due to proud, selfish, hard sinful hearts of leaders of nations. The orphan spirit was deep in the heart of our culture.

Since the Beginning of Creation

But the symptoms of our soul go deeper than this. In reality, the origin of the orphan heart goes back to the original sin in the heart of man. Up until then, Adam and Eve had true intimacy with God the Father. When they sinned they were separated from that intimacy and they started to act like orphans. Their sin also separated us from God and opened every subsequent generation to an orphan heart.

Genesis 3, verses 1-8 deal with their disobedience and their initial reaction. Then, when God called out to them and asked, 'Where are you?' (v.9), Adam's answer to God in verse 10 gives us insight to what had changed in his heart:

'I heard Your voice in the garden, and I was afraid because I was naked; and so I hid.'

Notice two things here:

First, he said they were afraid. They now acted as if they had never had intimacy with the Father. Instead of running to Him in their fear, they ran from Him. They sinned because they longed for their independence, but what they really needed was intimacy with the Father.

Second, he said that were afraid because they were naked. It wasn't just a physical nakedness. Something had shifted in their hearts too.

This is what the orphan heart does – it causes you to feel naked because you sense you are not covered; God's presence is not covering you. His peace and security are not palpable.

Nakedness causes a collective pulling away from God by estranged sons and daughters. Instead of being fathered – which enables them to be true fathers too, they become orphans. Orphans have no father covering them and are left to their own ways. They reproduce more orphans instead of sons and daughters of God.

The orphan reaction to this is to hide because they feel vulnerable and a lack security. Instead they look for things to replace their need for God the Father with other relationships. In our nation of Australia, it was mateship. A deep need for a sense of belonging. Men looked to their mates for a substitute for their need for intimacy. A 'drinking culture with mates blossomed.'* People looked for a sense of belonging elsewhere in clubs, sport, and mateship.

As we see here, the orphan heart is more than a person who had a difficult upbringing. It's actually a spirit that is transferred from generation to generation. So all nations today have multiple generations of orphans reproducing one after another. Orphan hearts cause a collective pulling away from God instead of moving towards Him. Orphans long

---

*The term "mateship" is quintessential Australian – it means 'you stand by your friends no matter what'.

for intimacy but only get a performance-based upbringing. There is not any reward of affection, assurance or encouragement. If you don't perform or measure up to an expectation, there is a constant withholding of approval. This is the heart of an orphan.

The problem is father figures who are broken will only act as orphans even though they should have learnt to love selflessly as fathers. They are still self-centered, controlling, emotionally immature, broken adults. The orphan heart is so strong that even when their children do well fathers can't tell them 'well done son/daughter'.

Genesis 3:10 describes the orphaned heart so well. It is what Restore the Foundation Ministry describes as 'shame, fear and control'.[1]

The Antidote

What can heal the hurting orphan heart? Genesis 4:26 gives us some insight–

'At that time people began to call on the name of the Lord'.

When you start to call on the Lord your focus changes from your orphan need to be loved on to the Father. When you begin to experience the love of God for the first time it causes a greater hunger in you for more of Him. When you truly experience the Father's love, the spirit of adoption comes on you. You become a son and daughter of God the Father.

This transforms your heart. Not only do you receive the spirit of adoption, you also get the spirit of reproduction. It shifts you from being a person who only reproduces orphans to someone who now reproduces sons and daughters.

The orphan spirit cannot express love. It cannot express emotion. Sadly, there are people in father roles in our society that have an orphan heart. How do I know? Because I have known them and used to be one, but now I am walking out of it. And you can too!

We need to realize that all of us have a little bit of orphan in us. It is a result of how our earthly fathers raised us and how other father figures like husbands, teachers, coaches, pastors, and others in authority treated us.

No one is better or worse than anybody else. We need to recognize and accept the truth that society today has an orphan spirit. This is the real reason why society is deteriorating. People don't care about others any more. The growing crime and drug problem is because of a distinct lack of fathering in our society.

Recently my adult children took me to a football game as a birthday present. After the game, on our way out we discovered that somebody had parked across the exit, blocking the exit out of the car park. Cars were trying to maneuver around this car but could not. I got out of our car and was helping others navigate around it. Cars could not exit for over 30 minutes. Eventually a group of young people who owned the car appeared. When others drew their attention to what that they had done, instead of being apologetic they became abusive. I reflected on this later and realized that this was a classic response of an orphan heart that had not been fathered. I was able to see with a father's heart what was really going on rather then get upset at them.

This is how we must respond when we are confronted with an orphan heart. We need to see with a father's eyes rather than react like an orphan too.

But there is an antidote!

It is to encounter the '*Father heart*' of God!

As we will discover in later chapters in more depth, it is possible to have a love encounter with the Father in which He transforms your heart with the spirit of sonship!

What makes this news even better is that the more we grow in the Father's heart the more it affects others around us. It creates hunger in others to also experience the love of the Father and it begins the journey of you changing from an orphan to a son.

I'm aware that many have had father figures in their lives who were abusive. I understand and there is no excuse for what they have done. It is never acceptable.

But there is an antidote and it starts with you inviting God the Father to reveal His Father's heart to you. This is the first step.

Allow the 'Father heart' of God to encounter you like never before.

ACTIVATION DECREE:

Stop for a moment. Get quiet in your thoughts.
Now ask God the Father,
'Let me have an intimacy encounter with you'.
'Reveal your father's heart to me'.
'Set me free. Deliver me from my orphan heart'.
'Father God, wrap your arms of love around me right now'.

Intimacy with God the Father is so important. It is foundational for our lives. This is clearly seen in Luke 1:17. It is the sequel to Malachi 4:5 – 6.

In Luke 1:11-16 an angel appears to John the Baptist's father, Zechariah, and prophesies over John the Baptist when he is still in Elizabeth's womb. He goes on in Luke 1:17 to prophesy a fulfillment of Malachi 4:5-6 over him where he decrees:

> 'He will also go before Him in the spirit and power of Elijah, 'to turn the hearts of the fathers to the children'.

John was sent by God to fulfil Malachi 4:5-6 – the turning of the hearts of the fathers to the children and the children's fathers!

Significantly he changes the last line of Malachi 4:5-6. Instead of prophesying, 'Or else I will come and strike the land with total destruction' he decrees:

'...To make ready a people prepared for the Lord'.

It means to prepare all us to encounter God intimately.

The way for us to live a supernatural life and fulfil our destiny is to have an intimacy encounter with God.

Get ready! His love for you will do just that as you read, prayer and encounter Him!

Activation Decree:

'I am ready to encounter you, God the Father.'

Please note that we use the term 'spirit of sonship' in a generic sense in this book. This is because of how it is presented in scripture. It is inclusive of both men and women. As it is a spiritual experience, it is possible for both sons and daughters to experience God's spirit of Sonship. We want everyone to feel included in this encounter.

Chapter 2

BECOMING SONS AND DAUGHTERS

Most self-help books, leadership training manuals, and mentoring lessons will have a component that helps you discover and embrace your identity. Some of these principles are valuable. However, it has been my experience that the only thing that causes true identity is a father's or mother's love and belief in you. God the Father longs for you to find yourself in Him by experiencing true sonship!

The prophet Isaiah saw this when he prophesied:

> 'I revealed myself to those who did not ask for me; I was found by those who did not seek me. To a nation that did not call on my name, I said, 'Here am I, here am I.'" – Isaiah 65:1

He finds us! He finds us and then reveals His intimate love to us – even when we are not looking for it. Then begins the process of truly and fully finding ourselves in Him.

"You Must Be Born Again"

It begins when we become born again which is the most important and essential step. We must all be born again.

Jesus said in John 3:3,

> 'Very truly I tell you no one can see the kingdom of God unless they are born again.'

He then goes on to explain what this means. In John 3:5 He again begins with the words 'very truly'. When Jesus says 'I'm telling you the truth' more than once in a conversation He is being very specific. And we need to listen very carefully to what He says next in John 3:5,

> 'Very truly I tell you no one can enter the kingdom of God unless they are born of water and the spirit. Flesh gives birth to flesh, but the spirit gives birth to spirit. You should not be surprised with me saying "you must be born again"'.

But there is more. John 3:13-16 tells us that this amazing spiritual experience is available to every person. The *'whoever believes in Him'* includes you if you make a decision to ask Jesus to take control of your life and for Him to take first place in your life and truly believe in Him as your Lord and Savior. Today is the day to make that decision if you have not done so yet.

'Now is the time of God's favor, now is the day of salvation' – 2 Corinthians 6:2.

ACTIVATION

If you have not asked Christ into your life already, why not take a moment and do that right now? There is a life changing prayer in the Endnotes of this book if you would like to go there now and pray.[1]

Salvation has favors and benefits that are out of this world. Not only do you receive the promise of eternal life, but you also get to live each day with Jesus your Savior and your Lord in intimate relationship. The transformation begins to be daily outworked in your life.

You start to truly live! You come alive to God and alive within yourself! You move from being self-centered to God and others-centered. Your life now has purpose and true meaning. You know the power of love, acceptance and forgiveness. As Paul says,

'The old has gone the new has come'.
– 2 Corinthians 5:17

You get to start your life again. It is the new you. The born-again you.

But there is another dimension available to every born-again believer that very few experience. When you are born again Jesus also opens the door of intimacy with God the Father for all His sons and daughters. Intimacy with the Father is for every born-again believer.

We No Longer Have to Be Orphans

'I will not leave you as orphans' – John 14:18a

Jesus also came so we no longer have to be orphans!

God's desire was to completely restore His relationship with humankind. Jesus is the door that begins with a spiritual born-again experience. Then Jesus also made a way for us to step into complete restoration of the intimacy that was destroyed in the garden when Adam and Eve sinned. When Jesus cried out on the cross *'it is finished'* a transformation process was also released for humankind called the spirit of sonship.

At salvation a metamorphosis process is begun. It is a supernatural transformation into the fullness of being sons and daughters of God.

Its immediate fruit is instant intimacy with the Father. It is a supernatural intimacy that cannot be naturally experienced. Jesus explained it this way:

"I will not leave you as orphans; I will come to you. Before long, the world will not see me anymore, but you will see me. Because I live, you also will live. On that day you will realize that I am in my Father, and you are in me, and I am in you.' – John 14:18-20

What did Jesus say? He said He is in us and we are in Him! It is hard to get your head around that!

In reality you are not meant to understand it but to experience it! The more you to step into your relationship of sonship with the Father, the more you will realize that *you are in the Father, and He is in you*!

Maybe you have heard the expression 'he is his father's son.' This means that the child has a striking resemblance to their father. Maybe it is a physical likeness, the way they speak, or even their personality. All in all, there is no mistaking to whom that person belongs.

However, Jesus takes it even a step further: Let's read verse 20 again:

'On that day you will realize that I am in my Father, and you are in me, and I am in you'.

Jesus declared that He is 'in' the Father so the Father and He are of one essence and substance. That awesome declaration states that Jesus is indeed part of the Father and the Father is part of Him. That in itself is remarkable. It opens up many dimensions of understanding of God and also eliminates the false belief that all gods are the same.

But Jesus didn't stop there. He goes on to say that when we are born again and truly step into our sonship that you and I are IN Jesus. When we truly realize this, it then can become our reality.

He also goes on to say that He is 'in' you. So like Jesus you are 'in' the Father and the Father is also 'in' you.

This is why He can be YOUR Father.

And why YOU are called His SON

The result of this revelation is remarkable. Not only with our intimacy – *In Him I am.* But also your identity - *In Him I see me.*

ACTIVATION DECREE:

Take a moment and decree:
'I am 'in' Christ'.
'I am in my Father, and He is in me, just as Christ is in me.'
'Thank you Father God that you are IN me'
'As I receive Christ the Savior and the Son, I also receive you Father in me'

Isn't this amazing? Now Jesus and the Father are both 'in' you.

This is why He can be YOUR Father.

And why YOU are called His SON/His DAUGHTER.

We will discover more about both your identity and intimacy with Him as sons and daughters in the following chapters.

Chapter 3

Intimacy with Father God

My wife and I have been married for over 35 years. We finished Bible College, got married, and went straight into full-time ministry. I was a pastor for twenty-eight of those years without ever encountering the Father heart of God.

I knew God the Father loved me but I had never experienced the Father's love in my heart. I used to hear Christians refer to God as 'Daddy God' and I wondered what planet they were on. In 1989 my family and I moved to America so I could attend Fuller Seminary and it was there that I heard a student refer to God that way. He had written a book on God as his father. He had been a professional football player and was a very striking young man. However, when he spoke about God He used terms like 'Daddy God'. This was very foreign to me. I didn't know what he was talking about as I had an orphan heart.

The reason for this was my poor relationship with my earthly father. All my years growing up my father had never expressed any love or emotion towards me. As a young boy I was desperate for his approval. This improved dramatically after I became a Christian but I still had an orphan heart.

When I heard my father was dying of cancer I tried to reach out to him a number of times without any results. God is always good so I did have the honor of leading my earthly father to Christ the day before he died. He cried as he asked Jesus Christ into his life. And I cried along with him. It was a mixture of joy that my earthly father was now saved but it was also the cry of a man who still needed to be loved by his father.

An Orphan Heart Healed

As a result of this orphan heart for many years nothing supernatural ever happened in my ministry. But all that changed after I visited Heidi Baker's ministry in Pemba, Mozambique.

There were children everywhere. It was chaotic. So many of the children were dirty and in ripped clothing. We discovered afterwards that the ones were who were clean were the ones Heidi had adopted while the ones that were dirty were village children. But regardless of what they looked like they all had one thing in common. They were loved unconditionally by Heidi and her team. The only way I can describe it was it was like liquid love. All the kids in the region wanted to hang out there. They have a school on the Iris base and all the children are welcome to attend.

Every Sunday they hold a church service at their base. During the service Heidi asks all the 'overseas' guests to come forward. Then they ask all the children to come forward and to pray for each adult.

I had two orphans praying for me. Cheryl and I have five children and we have taught each of our children how to pray publicly. As young children they typically had very short prayers. However, these children were not like that. They prayed and prayed for me. They didn't pray simple childlike prayers. They passionately interceded for me that I would experience God's father's heart. They asked the Father to bless me with His love.

Heidi Baker is never in a hurry. Her church services last from three to four hours. People walk for hours to attend so she has plenty of time and wants the children to take their time as they minister to guests. After ten minutes of them praying for me I realized that it was the first time in many years that someone had prayed for me for that long. I was very touched.

After fifteen minutes I began to weep. Up until then I had thought that they were the orphans; now I realized they weren't the orphans – I was! Then after 20 minutes of them praying intently for me I had a powerful supernatural experience – when you have a Father heart encounter the supernatural opens up to you.

In the spirit, I looked up to the ceiling of the church and saw a piece of paper floating down from the ceiling to me. I said out loud to God through my tears, 'What is that Father?' In reply I heard almost audibly, *'These are your adoption papers. Welcome home, son!'*

Something wonderful happened in my heart that day. From that time forward every thing in my life changed! I had encountered the 'Father heart' of God. I experienced God in a whole new way.

True Sons

Yes, I had known Jesus personally prior to this. He was my savior and my best friend. I lived for Him. However, even though I could recite Romans 8:14 – 16 by memory, I had never experienced it intimately:

> For all who are led by the Spirit of God are children of God.
>
> So you have not received a spirit that makes you fearful slaves. Instead, you received God's Spirit when he adopted you as his own children. Now we call him, 'Abba, Father'. For his Spirit joins with our spirit to affirm that we are God's children. (NLT)

I wasn't living it. I wasn't experiencing it.

I grew up in a Spirit-filled evangelical church. When a lot of my friends prayed they would yell at God. So I would pray that way too, especially when I was desperate. Even as a pastor on the way to church on Sunday morning, I would pray loudly, begging God to come and visit His people with power. After my Father heart experience, I realized that I had been praying out of desperation from an orphan heart. From that time forward my prayer life changed dramatically.

Now I was able to pray, 'Thank you, Papa God, that you love me and as a son of yours I know it's your good pleasure to give us all the kingdom. So would you pour out your Father's love today.'

This is how I live and minister now. I now make room for Him. I have learnt to flow in the Father's love. He loves to manifest the Holy Spirit's power.

I want to encourage you. There's a whole generation of adults trying to overcome fatherlessness. Because of this, now there's a whole new generation of fatherless children badly needing fathers and mothers to arise with the Father heart of God. There are Father heart encounters available to all of us.

As I began to grow into the understanding of God's Father's heart, I began to realize that our encounter with Him has no limit.

No Age Restriction

As mentioned in the Chapter 1, most people have some degree of an orphan spirit due to their upbringing. Some people have trouble relating to God as a loving Father because of this. As we've stated, many people have had painful experiences with harsh fathers or father figures. Often they were significant father figures like pastors, teachers, coaches who should have acted like fathers but did not. Instead they acted like orphans towards you when you were expecting a father's love. The good news is that it doesn't matter how old you are. Is not too late to experience the Father's love.

Even if you have been a Christian along time, the Lord sees your heart and wants to use you. He wants you to experience His intimate love so He can use you to share it with others. It will change the way you lead, train others and do ministry.

Once I experienced the Father's love, as a church we shifted from being program-focused to listening for the Father's voice and His leading. Instead of using church growth techniques we looked for what the Father was blessing and began to truly learn what Jesus said in John 5:19, 'I only do what I see the Father doing'.

Discipleship and mentoring is absolutely essential. But the basis of all discipleship must be to encounter God and know Him personally. This is what will motivate you every day for Gods' kingdom the rest of your life.

'For all who are led by the Spirit of God are sons of God...'

You can be true sons and daughters of God! Not just by name but by lifestyle.

Romans 8:15 says that the key is by 'Not receiving the spirit of slavery so that you live in fear again....'

God doesn't want you to live with an orphan heart, separated from Him. You were never destined to live this way. That was never His purpose. He always intended before the foundation of the world for you to live in intimacy with Him. It is time for you to step out of fear and slavery and to step into the freedom that only God the Father can give when you open your heart to Him and allow yourself to be delivered from an orphan spirit.

When that happens something wonderful begins in you. It will impact you so much that it will even cause your heart to cry out loud.

'...rather, the Spirit you received brought about your adoption to sonship. And by him we cry, "Abba, Father"'.

Just as a little baby cries out to his mother or father so as sons and daughters of God, we cry out to Him *'Abba Father.'*

The Father is truly revealed in you to such a degree that you call Him by His most intimate name – Abba or Papa Daddy! When this happens, something moves in your heart. It is the spirit of sonship! From that time forward you know that you know that you are a son, a daughter, of God the Father! Paul goes on to say...

'The Spirit himself testifies with our spirit that we are God's children.' – Romans 8:16

You have a witness inside your heart that you are no longer the same. You know who you are. And you know who your Father is. Immediately your intimacy with the father has led to your identity becoming fulfilled.

It is important to realize that the spirit of sonship is genderless. It is available to all, whether male or female. So when I speak of being a son of God the Father, all of us may experience this spirit of sonship.

The good news is that everyone is on a journey of growing in the spirit of sonship. The first step then is to experience Him as your 'Abba father'.

More good news. It is ageless, so it is for everyone. It doesn't matter how old or how young. It is for you!

Posture

As well as being ageless, to keep encountering God's Father's heart you need to have the right posture. Posture means you have to position yourself in a certain way. For a Christian it is a mental, emotional and spiritual attitude. I will share how to grow your posture in more depth in a later Chapter, 'How to Soar as Daddy's Child'.

It is important to first understand that it is possible for God's Father's heart to grow in us until our sonship reaches maturity. When that happens sons start to become fathers.

Paul says in 1 Corinthians 4:15,

'For you have many teachers in Christ but not many fathers'.

The classic example of this in the Bible is King David. In 2 Samuel 15 we see that David didn't start well as a father. He allowed his son Absalom to conspire and rebel against him as king for four years.

We don't do our children any favors when we allow them to disobey us. That is not being a loving parent. In fact, it is not modelling a true father's heart to them when we allow them to do that.

Absalom had a classic orphan heart. How can I be so sure?

2 Samuel 18:18 tells us that Absalom was only intent on building his own kingdom and not his father's kingdom. Verse 18 tells us that he built a monument to himself.

> 'During his lifetime Absalom had taken a pillar and erected it in the King's Valley as a monument to himself, for he thought, "I have no son to carry on the memory of my name." He named the pillar after himself, and it is called Absalom's Monument to this day'.

There is a growing trend in society today called *narcissism*. It is a lot different from having a good self-esteem or even a healthy acceptance of self. Narcissism is the extreme obsessive love of self that expresses itself in arrogance, self-importance, self-focus, superiority over others, and self-centeredness. It is the ultimate example of a fully developed orphan heart.

Absalom had all of these things operating in his life. He had a fully developed orphan heart. He was so obsessed with himself that he was even prepared to kill his own father so he could become king of Israel. Thankfully that didn't happen. Orphan hearts accuse, undermine and even try and destroy true fathers. While David had to initially run for his life, eventually Absalom was killed and David remained king and Israel was saved.

Acts 13:22 tells us that God decreed over David before he became king,

> 'I have found David son of Jesse, **a man after my own heart**; he will do everything I want him to do.' (Bold added).

God knew the posture of David's heart. It was a heart after God's own heart. David had discovered the Father heart of God. He desired above all things to please God more than anything else. Even though he wasn't a good father as a young dad with his son Absalom, God knew David had the potential of growing into a **great father because of the posture of his heart towards God.**

Towards the end of David's life, we see something wonderful had happened. He grew into a great father.

In 1 Chronicles 22:5 we are told that by the time Solomon was of age David had learnt to be a great father and had grown a mature father's heart.

> 'David said, "My son Solomon is young and inexperienced, and the house to be built for the Lord should be of great magnificence and fame and splendor in the sight of all the nations. Therefore I will make

preparations for it" So David made extensive preparations before his death.'

It so important that we have the right posture when it comes to the Father heart of God. David was a man after God's own heart. We can too if we have the right posture!

Reality

The truth is that you can hear all this incredible teaching on the Father heart of God but never apply to it to your life.

You can even have great spiritual father figures in your life but if you don't allow them to help you to grow as a son, the reality is that you will struggle to become free from the orphan spirit.

The parable of the Prodigal son in the gospel of Luke 15 is a great illustration of this.

We can learn a lot from the father in this story. He was a really good father with a true father's heart. He had two sons. The youngest one wanted his inheritance *now*. Before he was ready. The father didn't hesitate and gave it to him. The son squandered all of his inheritance.

The father never stopped loving the son who had taken all his inheritance prematurely, yet he refused to go and rescue the son out of the pigpen. Ultimately, this is what caused the prodigal son to wake up to himself. We too need to learn to refuse to rescue our sons and daughters when they won't listen and allow them to experience the consequences of their life decisions. Rescuing them at every turn does not help them grow up as sons and daughters. It ultimately restricts them from becoming free from the orphan heart and becoming good fathers and mothers with the Father heart of God.

Luke 15:17-19 tells us that the prodigal actually turned his heart toward home. He turned his heart back to his father. He knew he needed his father.

> When he came to his senses, he said, 'How many of my father's hired servants have food to spare, and here I am starving to death! I will set out and go back to my father and say to him: Father, I have sinned against heaven and against you. I am no longer worthy to be called your son; make me like one of your hired servants.'

This young man was so desperate that he was even prepared to give up his sonship and become a servant of the Father. But we are created to be a son of God not a slave for God.

When we hold Father Heart Encounters, I always ask this question:

If you could live in a lovely home with a lovely loving family would you rather be a son or a servant?

Without fail people always answer *A son.* Why? Because we all have a desire to be a son or a daughter in a family with a loving father and mother. How much more can we be a son or a daughter of our loving Father God!

Even though the youngest son was wrong and had sinned and wasted all his inheritance, the father still kept loving him. When he turned his heart toward home, Luke 15:20 tells us,

> 'But while he was still a long way off, his father saw him and was filled with compassion for him; he ran to his son, threw his arms around him and kissed him.'

I believe the father never stopped looking for his son. Every day he would stand watching, looking, believing, expecting that his son eventually would realize he was better off in his father's house.

What did the father do when he saw his son coming home? He was filled with compassion – he ran to his son. He ran to his son even before he had arrived home – even before his son had repented. Verse 21 tells us that the son humbled himself and said to his father,

> 'Father, I have sinned against heaven and against you. I am no longer worthy to be called your son.'

While we teach that we should humble ourselves and turn to God, this is a wonderful picture of God's Father heart towards us. When we turn our heart toward home, God doesn't wait until we've finished our prayer. God the Father runs to us. He runs to us with open arms.

The father saw the turning of the son's heart and it caused him to run in love to him. This is what Daddy God does for us today and every day of our lives too.

'Yes my son, my daughter, I love you. Welcome home! Welcome home son! Welcome home daughter. You are loved. I love you. I love you'

When he was still a long way off, the father saw him. The father was filled with compassion and ran to his son and kissed him. The father didn't just kiss him once. He kissed him and kissed him and kissed him!

What did the father of the prodigal son do? He loved his son unconditionally.

The father refused to reject his son even though he had sinned. Instead the father did just the reverse. He took the best robe and a ring and sandals and clothed his son with a father's love and they celebrated.

Are You a Prodigal?

The truth is there are two prodigals in that story. We always focus on the son that left. But the son that stayed behind was an orphan as well as he didn't know what truly belonged to him.

Luke 15:31 says this to him and to us today,

'My son,' the father said, 'you are always with me, and everything I have is yours.

Most Christians don't know what truly belongs to them. They don't know that what belongs to the Father belongs to them. How can I be so sure? Because I lived that way. Orphans are always focusing on what's missing or what they need from God instead of what they already have from Him.

We need to truly believe that we have everything we need for life and godliness because the Father loves us.

He Longs for You

In many ways we are all prodigals until we encounter the spirit of adoption! We are sons and daughters who are 'away' from the father in our hearts, self-image and what we see in others.

Just like the father in this parable, the Father sees you today. He is looking for you and He is longing for you to turn your heart to a deeper encounter with Him as your loving, heavenly Father.

This story is a wonderful picture of God's Father heart towards us. He runs to us today with His arms wide open! His arms are always wide open. Learn to lean into His heart and hear His heartbeat of love for you.

There is a new level of encounter of the Father's heart in the body of Christ right now. This message has been powerfully taught for a number of decades since the 1980s but there is a new emphasis on the 'Father heart of God' again.

Many wonderful fathers like the late Robert Frost and John Arnott have been imparting this for years. There seems to be a second wave being released by the Father now.

God is calling you into a whole new level of intimacy with Him. And out of that intimacy flow your identity and authority. I sense there is a new commissioning of the Father's heart message for you to carry.

We are in a season of God restoring all things! This especially includes the Father heart of God.

It starts with us right now. The key way to encounter God the Father is through humility and hunger for Him.

Activation questions:

Are you willing to be humble and hungry for more of God's love?

Do you truly want to experience His Father's heart for you?

Pray:

Father, thank you this opportunity to humble ourselves before you. We ask you to forgive us for living like an orphan and not a son/daughter. We turn our heart toward you. We are hungry for more of your unconditional love. I ask that you would set me free from any orphan spirit. Free me now. Reveal your Father's love to me. Thank you that nothing that will separate me from your love. I ask that you would adopt me as your son/daughter today. I see you running towards me now with open arms. I decree I am now safe at home in my father's house of love. – In Jesus name. Amen

If you have a prodigal son or a daughter away from God today, Pray this prayer. It works: *'Turn their hearts toward home today. Let them see they're better off on in their father's house. In Jesus' name'.*

Intimacy with the Father Is Possible

God knows us intimately! And He wants us to know Him intimately. Often people ask me if it is possible to know God this way. I always answer the same way - absolutely!

The Word of God confirms this in Psalms 139:1,2:

> 'You have searched me, Lord, and you know me. You know when I sit and when I rise; you perceive my thoughts from afar.'

David knew God intimately. He says in verse 13,

> 'For you created my inner being; you knit me together in my mother's womb…'

…and in verse 16,

> 'Your eyes saw my unformed body; all the days ordained for me were written in your book before one of them came to be.'

The apostle Paul prayed for us in Ephesians 1:17 that all believers would 'know God' this way. He prayed,

> 'I keep asking that the God of our Lord Jesus Christ, the glorious Father, may give you the Spirit of wisdom and revelation, so that you may know him better.'

The truth is you can know someone by name and even be on speaking terms with them yet not truly know them. In the West we often say we 'know' somebody but in fact, we don't know them at all. What does Paul mean when he talks about knowing God? Paul is saying it is possible to have an intimate relationship with God. When someone told me that as young man, I had trouble comprehending it. How could that be? The answer of course is through God's son Jesus Christ. He has made a way for you and me to go past all the ceremony and restrictions into a deep place of relationship and intimacy with God the Father.

True relationships are not a one-way path. If you were married to someone who only spoke to you when they were upset or in crisis and never stopped to listen to what you had to say, I can imagine you would decide it wasn't much of a marriage. Yet that describes most people's relationship with God. Most people when they pray only use a monologue without ever stopping to listen to what God has to say to them.

It is possible to have an intimate relationship with God the Father. How intimate? The same type of intimacy as a husband and wife. Now I'm not talking merely about a sexual intimacy. Often when my wife and I are in a large group of people in a party setting and we are in different parts of the room, when our eyes meet I can just make a facial expression and she knows exactly what I'm thinking. I can look at her in a certain way and she nods in reply knowing immediately that it's time to go. Perhaps I raise my eyebrows in a certain way and she will laugh even though no words are being spoken to each other. Why? Because she knows exactly what I'm thinking. I think most couples who know each other well relate together this way. It is because we have spent a lot of time with each other building relationship. We know how to listen and to communicate with each other.

The basis of true relationship is always love. When you love someone you begin to know that person intimately.

1 Corinthians 8:3 says,

'But whoever loves God is known by God.'

So to love God is to truly know Him.

Intimacy-> Identity-> Authority-> Release

Intimacy with God is essential. Without intimacy you will never truly discover your true identity.

But there is more.

Bill Johnson teaches that intimacy is also the basis of our authority. I've discovered that those with great spiritual authority always know who they are in Christ. Not only are they confident of their identity in Him but they also have an ongoing intimate relationship with God the Father. As I was meditating on this truth I discovered something else that happens in us because of intimacy with God the Father. Those that teach spiritual formation refer to a convergence that takes place in a Christian's life when they begin to move out of intimacy and identity with authority into great fruitfulness. It is like a 'release' or an overflow of identity and authority expressed through, love, effectiveness, and brings fulfilment in a person's life.

We have a friend who is an emerging leader of a very effective drug rehabilitation program in our city. It has been a great joy to see him grow in his character, leadership, authority and effectiveness in only a few years. I continue to be blessed at the release of life that flows through him to others. It is wonderful to see people with addictions step into freedom and come alive. I love the way their countenance changes as they encounter God. Their faces actually shine and their eyes are filled with life and freedom.

But it wasn't always that way for our young friend. He also comes from a life of addiction and abuse. It's been a joy to see him discover the Father's love and step into his identity and begin to exercise authority in Christ. The release in his life is now overflowing into others and releasing them to do the same.

Intimacy with God the Father is so important. There is nothing you can do that will ever separate you from His love.

Romans 8:38-39 says,

And I am convinced that nothing can ever separate us from God's love. Neither death nor life, neither angels nor demons, neither our fears for today nor our worries about tomorrow—not even the powers of hell can separate us from God's love. No power in the sky above or in the earth below—indeed, **nothing** in all creation **will ever be able to separate us from the love of God** that is revealed in Christ Jesus our Lord. - NLT (Bold added.)

Activation Decree:

'Nothing can ever separate me from God's love'.

If you don't have a personal relationship with God the Father, you may struggle to understand what true intimacy with God is. What changed most for me after I had that encounter with the Father in Mozambique in 2008 was my prayer life. I am a light sleeper so I'm often awake during the night. Before encountering the 'Father heart' of God, I would lie awake worrying or thinking so much that I couldn't go back to sleep. Now when I am awake, I have learnt just to lean in to my heavenly Father. I step straight into intimacy with the words, *I love you Father – Papa God* and immediately I hear him say back, *I love you too son*. His presence always comes in that instant. I sense His amazing and unconditional love. Often I'm caught up for long periods of time in His presence. The fruit of these times are always amazing. I experience such a great sense of being His Son and knowing exactly how He wants me to live and what He wants me to do.

Activation:

Choose to step into intimacy with the Father now. Try using the words, 'I love you, Daddy God' or similar. Use your holy imagination to see Him with His arms around you, holding you and saying, 'I love you too son', 'I love you too daughter'.
Meditate on this and say it over and over a number of times. Something wonderful will begin to happen inside of you.

Chapter 4

BECAUSE OF HIS LAVISH LOVE...

Your Father not only loves you, He also delights in lavishing His love on you. *Lavish* is not a word we use often today but it is a powerful and beautiful word.

1 John 3:1 says,

'What great love the Father has LAVISHED on us...'

To lavish means *'to expend or give in great amounts; without limit; to bestow in abundance or shower.'*

The great news is that the Lord *lavishes* His love on you! This means that there is no limit to the love the Father lavishes on you today and every day.

Unwrapping this Lavish Gift

Every year in our family we have the tradition of placing a Christmas tree in our lounge room. The week leading up to Christmas, at the base of the tree the presents grow steadily in number. We now have such a large extended family and growing number of grandchildren there seem to be more and more guests – and henceforth gifts – every year on Christmas day. A few years ago I received more gifts than usual. Due to the large volume of gift paper being unwrapped, I overlooked one of my smaller gifts. It had been placed in the pile of new clothes and other items that I'd been given. I only discovered it a few days later as I was getting ready for the new year. I sensed the Holy Spirit teaching me that a gift is only truly received once it is unwrapped and put to use.

This amazing love has been given to us. Yet we have to receive it. We have to unwrap it in our lives before it will become a reality in us.

When we meditate on the fact that God wants to lavish His love on us, it seems like it should be the other way around. He is the worthy One! He should be having all the love lavished on Him! But instead, He has lavished His love on us.

Why does He do this? 1 John 3:1 tells us why:

'See what great love the Father has lavished on us, that we should be called children of God!'

Why? So *we* can become *the children of God.*

Now you might be saying as you read this, *'Yes, Yes, Yes… I already know I am God's Child!'*

But do you truly know the type of love that practically transforms you from being an orphan to an actual son or daughter? Let's delve more into this.

The Spirit of Sonship

In Romans 8:14-15, the Greek word for 'adoption to sonship,' *huiothesia,* is a legal term referring to the full legal standing of an adopted male heir that was used in Roman culture. At that time it was a big deal to be a Roman citizen and even bigger deal to be the male heir.

In researching this book, I discussed this term with my friend Brian Simmons, a wonderful Bible translator who is fluent in biblical Greek and Hebrew and is author of *The Passion Translation* of the Bible. I also had a wonderful discussion with my spiritual mother Patricia King concerning the use of this term. They both said the same thing – that the English word 'adoption' is not the best translation for this term. The more correct translation is the *'spirit of sonship'* in place of the 'spirit of adoption'.

There is much more to the 'spirit of sonship'.

When you receive the 'spirit of sonship', your DNA actually changes so that you receive the same DNA as your Father. You actually become His child. You truly become a son of God! This is not the same in the case of an orphan who is adopted by an earthly father and mother. When you are adopted you might change your name to your father's name but you still have your birth mother and father's DNA.

When you receive the '*spirit of sonship*' you are more than adopted, you are so loved by the Father *that you become like Him* in every way.

I love seeing older married couples who have been married for decades and are obviously still in love. They have loved each other so strongly that their physical appearance changes and *they end up looking like each other*. Likewise, when you receive the *'spirit of sonship'* and allow the father to lavish His love on you, you begin to become like Him! You reflect His love others wherever you go.

It gets even better. When we truly experience the spirit of sonship our relationship with God moves in a number of amazing ways.

Our relationship moves *from:*

>...always trying to PLEASE father figures. The bottom line is the harder you try the more you will fall short

>...serving Him out of EXPECTATION – including religious expectations

>...serving Him out of OBLIGATION

>...pleasing Him out of FEAR. Paul describes moving from the *'spirit of slavery to fear'*.

We move *into* ...

>...knowing that He loves you unconditionally as His sons and daughters

>...knowing Him as your *Papa Daddy, our Abba Father!*

>...desiring to please and serve Him becomes a natural response to His love

We Move *into* His Set Time

Paul says it this way in Galatians 4:4:

>But when the <u>set time</u> had fully come, God sent his Son, born of a woman, born under the law, to redeem those under the law, that we might receive adoption to sonship. Because you are his sons, God sent the Spirit of his Son into our hearts, the Spirit who calls out, 'Abba, Father.' So you are no longer a slave, but God's child; and since you are his child, God has made you also an heir. (Underline added.)

Paul tells that us at the 'set time' God sent His Son. Now it is the 'set time' again but now He is sending us - His 'sons and daughters' of God! By His spirit of sonship you are now able to come into the fullness of who you are here on earth to live as His son or daughter!

His *set time* has come for you and it is right now! You need to step into it!

Entering into the Spirit of Sonship

How does this transformation of sonship happen? Through the exercise of the same gift of faith that Abraham had in his life. And that faith is yours too. All you have to do is *accept* that fact and then *believe in faith*!

Let's dig into Scripture to help us grasp this profound truth:

We are children of God through faith

Galatians 3:26,27:

'So in Christ Jesus you are ALL children of God through faith.... For ALL of you who were baptized into Christ have clothed yourselves with Christ' (uppercase added).

All means ALL. There are no exceptions. It means you too!

When you are born again, you are 'baptized into His death.'

Romans 6:3:

'Or don't you know that all of us who were baptized into Christ Jesus were baptized into his death?'

'Baptized into His death' means that you die to your old self; this means your DNA dies too.

We are not only buried with Him, but also brought into new life.

Romans 6:4:

We were therefore buried with him… into death in order that, just as Christ was raised from the dead through the glory of the Father, we too may live a new life.

This new life means you are now 'clothed with Christ', with the same DNA that Jesus had.

Galatians 3: 27:

For ALL of you who were baptized into Christ have clothed yourselves with Christ'. (Uppercase added.)

You are now clothed with the same DNA of the spirit of sonship that Jesus had when He was here on earth. Wow! This is incredible. You truly become His son, His daughter!

Galatians 3:28 reinforces this*:*

'There is neither Jew nor Gentile, neither slave nor free, nor is there male and female, for you are ALL ONE in Christ Jesus'.(Upper case added.)

You are no longer 'of man's seed'. Something in your DNA has changed!

You are no longer the same person born as an orphan separated from your Father God!

Paul describes you this way in Galatians 3:29,

IF you belong to CHRIST, then you are Abraham's SEED, and heirs according to the promise. (Upper case added,)

You are no longer an orphan! Your seed has changed. You now have the seed or DNA of a son or a daughter of God!

Just recently I watched the story of a young boy from Ethiopia who had been adopted by an Australian family when he was four years old. He had come from extreme poverty. After his father died from malnutrition, his mother could no longer care for him so she gave him up for adoption.

Six years later I saw him perform on a talent show in front of 2000 people in Australia. He had such a beautiful smile and was so full of confidence. His music was good and he was very talented for his age. But the thing that impressed me the most was his adoptive mother's statement to him before he walked on stage. *You know that whatever happens out there on that stage you are just as great now as you will be when you walk off that stage.* His response was, *Mom is so proud of me.* He was right. His mother was beaming with love and pride for her adopted son.

But you are more than an adopted son or daughter – you are a true son and daughter of God. So how much more is God the Father in love with you and is proud of you!

It gets even better –

If you are a true son or a daughter, then you are an heir!

Occasionally in the media there are court cases where the children of a deceased millionaire are contesting the will of their deceased father because they have not been included in the inheritance. On paper it would seem that they would have no right to their father's estate because they were not specifically mentioned in his will as a beneficiary, so many would argue that they should not inherit anything. However, often they receive a judgment in their favor. Why? Because they are the son or daughter and they have their father's DNA. Because of his DNA they have a right to be an heir! So they want what truly belongs to them as a son or daughter – their inheritance!

The good news is you are not just any son or daughter. You are sons and daughters of Abba Father! The Father of all fathers! The God of all gods!

We will discuss this further in a later chapter.

Results And Evidence Of Sonship

When we are born-again of incorruptible seed we have been transformed by the spirit of sonship.

This is not a figment of your imagination or an abstract concept. This is a real practical, tangible transformation!

It is a real and actual spiritual experience that you can and must have.

The first thing that happens is that you have immediate intimacy with God the Father.

'Because you are his sons, God sent the Spirit of his Son into our hearts, the Spirit who calls out, 'Abba', Father' – Galatians 4:6

It is immediate because you instantly sense His overwhelming acceptance and limitless love.

Because it is intimate you can hear His voice more clearly than you ever could previously. I share more about this later. It is a heart-to-heart connection that compares to nothing else you can ever experience. His deep, limitless love instantly is revealed into your heart.

Second, your identity changes very dramatically as you have become His Child.

You become His beloved son, His beloved daughter – to the degree that when reading Luke 3:22 it is not presumptuous to superimpose your name in place of the name of the Son of God!!

'And a voice came from heaven: 'You are my Son, whom I love; with you I am well pleased." Luke 3:22

Your sonship is that powerful! It is that real! It is that WONDERFUL. Why don't you declare it right now!

ACTIVATION DECREE:

Decree this out loud over yourself-
'I am His son/daughter'.
'I am His precious son/daughter'.
'I am His precious son whom He loves'.
'I am His precious son with whom He is well pleased'.

As you decree that powerful revelation, I sense Him declaring over you...
'You are MY son/daughter'.
'You are MY son/daughter' whom I love'.
'I AM pleased with you"

Something wonderful happens inside you when you get this revelation. Deep in your heart you begin to truly believe that 'I am HIS son/ HIS daughter'.

Over and over again you hear Him saying 'I love you. I love you. I love you.'

Allow this to sink deeply into your soul!

Allow Him to reveal just who you have really become!

You are HIS SON ... His PRECIOUS SON.

You are HIS DAUGHTER.... His PRECIOUS DAUGHTER.

Decree it out loud

'I am HIS!'
Not just any son/ daughter, but His precious son/ daughter!
'I am HIS son/ daughter'

But what does it mean to be a true son or daughter? In the next chapter we will explore this further.

Chapter 5

Your Identity as His Son

When you experience the Father's love you begin to receive a true revelation of your identity in Christ as His son.

Those who struggle with their identity often may be able to point back to their childhood or growing up when a parent or a father figure failed them in some way. The outcome was it undermined their true identity.

Something that is missing in Western society is the celebration of children moving into adulthood. In the Hebrew culture they still have an initiation ceremony for boys who reach the age of 13 called a bar mitzvah. It is the recognition that a boy has become a man and can begin to be treated as an adult. Not only does the ceremony signify they are ready to participate in public worship but that they are also ready to begin to live as an adult, even on behalf of the family.

In Jesus' time, after the equivalent of a boy's bar mitzvah, the father would take his son into the marketplace. The father would climb on to a high section of the marketplace and get the attention of all those present.

He would then declare something like this: 'This is my son who I love and with whom I'm well pleased. He is now a man. From now on when my son speaks, he speaks for me. When my son enters into business transactions, he is doing so with my full authority. What belongs to me belongs to him. When he gives his word it's as if I am giving my word'.

Jesus had a similar experience at His water baptism – we briefly touched on this previously. In Luke 3:21-22 we are told that when Jesus was baptized, heaven was opened and the Holy Spirit physically descended on Him in the form of a dove. As a pastor, I prepared people for their own water baptism with this passage of Scripture for many years. I always taught them to expect the Holy Spirit to come upon them as they are baptized in water. But I now realize I was only teaching them half of what happened to Jesus at His baptism.

Luke 3:22 goes on to say,

'And a voice came from heaven: "You are my son, whom I love; with you I am well pleased"'.

The Bible tells us that all present heard the Father's voice that day. Everyone present heard what He said to His son. The power and significance of this was not lost on them that day.

Imagine for a moment how Jesus must have felt as He heard His Father say to Him, '*You are my son whom I love; with you I'm well pleased.*' Jesus would have felt so loved and affirmed by His Father. His identity was fulfilled that day into the fullness of the Son of Man. He knew who He was, and knew that He had all authority in heaven and earth because His Father loved Him and said so!

We have already seen that Romans 8:14–16 tells us that if we are led by the Spirit of God we too are sons and daughters of God and we know Him as our Father. So the Father is declaring the same thing over you today:

'*You are my son / my daughter whom I love; with you I'm well pleased.*'

He is pleased with you! He loves you! And He decrees this audibly over you today too.

ACTIVATION DECREE:

'*He is pleased with me.*'

When you come to the realization that Father God loves you and is pleased with you, then something wonderful happens on the inside of your heart.

As a young man I heard a famous Christian leader say, 'When I sit down after I have finished preaching I always pray, "I hope I pleased you today, God"'. I was impressed by that and began to do the same thing whenever I preached. I continued this practice as a senior pastor, praying that way after I finished leading a church service. I thought it was something that would please God and keep me humble at the same time. But after experiencing the love of the Father I began to read the scripture in a whole different light. It was like 'orphan scales' dropped off my eyes. Whenever I would read His Word I would see how much the Father loved me. I read how the Father truly sees His son and daughters. I realized that He is already pleased with me.

And He is already pleased with you. Isn't that wonderful? He is pleased with you! You don't have to perform to please Him.

Activation Decree:

Close your eyes for a moment now and let that wash over you.
Listen! He is saying it over you right now!
'You are my son / my daughter whom I love'.
'I'm pleased with you'.
Repeat it again: *'He is pleased with me. My Father is pleased with me'.*

Sons And Daughters Are Led by His Spirit

One of the keys to living in your identity as a son or a daughter of Daddy God the Father is to be led by His Spirit everyday. We have already touched on this briefly, but let's examine it now more in depth:

'For those who are led by the Spirit of God are the children of God.' – Romans 8:14,

What does it mean to be led by the Spirit of God?

I've learned that when you truly fall in love, it is a natural response to want to please that person in return. When you experience the love of the Father all you want to do is to love Him more. One of the ways that you can grow in your love toward the Father is to learn to listen for the voice of the Holy Spirit and to follow His leading. He will lead you, and the more you listen, the more you follow. His voice and your perception will become clearer. The more you learn to be led by the Spirit, the more you grow up as a son and daughter of God.

The Bible also calls this living a holy life. As a younger Christian, I would always struggle with holiness because it seemed that no matter how hard I tried, I felt I was never good enough. Since I encountered the Father heart of God and His amazing love, I simply choose to please Him – the One who loves me. I've found that this results in so much more holiness than all my previous efforts. I choose to love Him more and more. You can too.

Choosing to be led by the Spirit every day had ramifications in many areas of my life. Something else that changed dramatically after my Father heart experience was the way we did ministry. Prior to that experience we were 'purpose driven' by programs and strategies. We would teach on the power of vision and how to implement goals through strategies. While we had some success, most of the time we found ourselves falling short of what we hoped to achieve. After having my heart transformed, we began to follow Jesus' example more and more. This spilled over into how we did ministry. We read what Jesus said in John 5:19,

> 'I only do what I see my father doing'.

We learned very quickly to begin to look and see what the Father was blessing in our ministry. So instead of doing everything that was expected in church life, we learnt to begin to focus our energy and resources on what the Father was blessing. We called it 'looking for the oil.' Our church was an inner-city church that would reach out to the unemployed, homeless and elderly. We began a feeding program that provided lunches for those who are destitute and poor. It became quickly obvious that this was the heart of the Father. By the second week, thirty people were lining up in the rain for a hamburger lunch. Rather than spreading our energy over many ministries, we began to concentrate on this one.

The favor of God flowed freely. We were given a number of new motor vehicles, large commercial sized freezers and cold rooms. Many people started to come to Christ and be healed and free from addictions. They soon became our volunteers. We always declared that the lunch was free but it cost those who came five minutes of their time to listen to a testimony of a person's life changed by Christ.

The blessing of God continued to increase on our care program. Eventually we were feeding up to 250 people a day and giving away three tons of food a week. The city council and state government became aware of what we were doing and we were offered funding for different employment programs and housing initiatives to help people find work and accommodation.

One day an older lady in our congregation approached me about the possibility of starting a thrift shop at our church in a spare storeroom. I explained I was happy for her to go ahead if she mobilized others. I also asked her to use donations to run the shop explaining that the budget of the church was already committed. Within a short period of time we discovered that more people were coming to Christ and being added to the church through those elderly volunteers staffing that thrift shop than anything else our care program was doing. While we had many wonderful people helping run this amazing outreach program, the basis of it all was that we had learned to see what the Father was blessing and were willing to challenge our energy in those things.

Led into the Wilderness…

I've discovered that if you are willing to be led by the Spirit of God you will be led into the most amazing and even unusual places.

We see in Luke 4:1 that even Jesus, 'Full of the Holy Spirit…. was led by the spirit into the wilderness'

What happened immediately after His glorious baptism experience? He was led by the Spirit into the wilderness. It has been my experience that often after amazing glory experiences the next step is often into wilderness. But I have discovered that there is glory in the wilderness too. We will talk more about that in a later chapter.

It's important for us to realize that how we respond when we are led by the Spirit into the wilderness determines the level of kingdom authority we walk in. It's important not to be afraid of the wilderness. This is where we learn power and authority. As a boy, David learnt to kill the lion and the bear when he was in the wilderness caring for His father's sheep. The wilderness prepared him not to be afraid of giants and how to cut off their heads.

I often hear Christians praying, 'Lord, make me like you' and, 'Let your will be done in my life'. But when the Spirit of God answers that prayer by leading them into wilderness and hardship they complain and say, 'Lord what are you doing to me?' God's answer is always the same - 'I am answering your prayers when you pray 'Lord, make me like you'.'

Being led by the Spirit of God as sons and daughters often means we are led into the wilderness by Him. Look what happened to Jesus after He went into the wilderness where He was tempted but did not sin.

'Jesus returned to Galilee in the power of the Holy Spirit…' – Luke 4:14

He came out of the wilderness full of the power of the

Holy Spirit. When you see with the Father's eyes the same thing will happen to you.

The realm of the supernatural becomes a reality.

Sons and Daughters Experience Power and Authority

The power and authority of the Holy Spirit increase in your life dramatically once you start to live as a son of God. The more your identity flows out of intimacy with the Father, the more His authority manifests in your life. This is the key to living in the power and authority of the Spirit everyday. You must learn to lean into His heart. As you do this you will grow in being led by the Spirit of God and the supernatural will manifest more and more.

Just recently we were travelling with our spiritual mother Patricia King in Western Africa. One day my wife and I had to fly from Ghana to Mali. We were travelling in a small aircraft that had about 30 passengers – a turbo propeller plane. Soon after taking off we hit the worst storm I've ever encountered. It was so severe that our aircraft was struck with lightning a number of times. The whole plane was shaking and vibrating violently. Luggage was falling out of overhead lockers. Suddenly the plane dropped. We instantly fell hundreds of feet. This happened at least three times in a row. Passengers were screaming and crying loudly. Some were shouting, '*We are going to die*!'. I turned and saw the flight attendant with his head in his hands shaking and crying so I realized that this was a very serious situation. But my wife Cheryl and I were not afraid. We had this amazing peace in our hearts. I said to her, *'I don't sense this is the day we are going to die. But these people sure think so.'* Immediately, I sensed the Holy Spirit say that I needed to preach the gospel and lead those people to Christ who thought they were dying. So that is what I did. I raised my voice and shouted loudly over all the crying, *'Listen to me. You need to make peace with God right now. You need to ask Jesus Christ to come into your life and take control so you can be sure that you will go to heaven if you die today. You need to pray this prayer after me.'*

I began to pray out loud and told them to repeat what I was saying. After we finished praying, the number of people screaming seemed to settle down. The plane was still shaking violently. We were still being hit by lightning causing loud noise all around us. We had been travelling like this now for over twenty minutes. The plane dropped suddenly again and passengers screamed. I looked at Cheryl and said, *'We need to speak to this storm.'*

So that is what we did. We prayed like Jesus prayed when he was in the boat with the disciples in the midst of the storm. After three minutes of praying with authority over the storm, the plane fell one more time. However, this time it fell out of the storm into still blue sky. The passengers applauded and cheered out loud. The pilot then made an announcement. He apologised for what had just happened. He advised us that because we were flying in such a small plane he didn't have the equipment to detect such a severe storm. He added that in thirty years of flying that was the worst storm he had ever flown through.

When I have shared this story with other Christians, often they are amazed at how Cheryl and I responded so calmly in the face of very dangerous circumstances. But I don't think that we are better Christians than anybody else or have some amazing gift of faith. We simply have discovered who we are as sons and daughters of God. So can you.

As Sons and Daughters, The kingdom of God Is Inside You

When you know who your Father is and that you are His son or daughter, then you know that everything that belongs to Him belongs to you. You begin to believe that everything in the kingdom of God is available to you. In fact, the kingdom of God is already inside you.

Jesus said that in Luke 17:20-21,

Now when He was asked by the Pharisees when the kingdom of God would come, He answered them and said, 'The kingdom of God does not come with observation; nor will they say, 'See here!' or 'See there!' For indeed, the kingdom of God is within you.'

Did you get that? The kingdom of God is already within you! So many pray for more and more of God's glory but they don't realise that they already have the kingdom of heaven within them. They already have it. If you are born again by the Spirit of God, you too have the kingdom of God inside you. And when you know you're adopted by your heavenly Father and are led by His Spirit, then the kingdom of God will powerfully flow through you to others and to change the circumstances around you.

Most Christians don't truly know what's inside them. How do I know that? Because of the way they speak and live.

Soon after my eldest daughter was married, she came to visit my wife and me one day. I was working in my office at home and Cheryl was in our house of prayer which we have on our property. My daughter opened the front door and called out her greetings to us. But then I didn't hear anything else and I assumed that she had gone to see my wife in our house of prayer. However, I heard a noise in our kitchen, which surprised me, so I went to investigate. There was my daughter with our fridge open eating our food. Now she had own house and her own food. But she was eating our food without asking our permission. But I was not upset. In fact, I was very blessed, because I realised my daughter knew that what belonged to her father belong to her!

Immediately, I saw the power of this example for all Christians. When we truly experience our Father's love, we know that we are His son or daughter. We also know that what belongs to God the Father belongs to us as His sons and daughters. So out of our intimacy with the Father comes our identity. And out of our identity as sons and daughters comes our spiritual authority.

How long does it take to become intimate with God? You can instantly go there. It doesn't matter whether you are in a car, at home or at work you can be intimate with Him. Even in the midst of pain and trouble you can know this intimacy. There is also wonderful fruit that grows in you. I find that as I grow as a son I don't react to a sudden change of circumstances and act as an orphan nearly as much any more. There is so much more peace and a sense that Daddy God is in control even when life does not make sense. The other joy of encountering God as your Father is that it changes your prayer life dramatically. You will move from being a servant and subject to your circumstances to being a son or daughter of Daddy God.

The Father Heart of God Will Begin to Grow in You

The more you encounter God as your Father, the Father heart of God begins to grow in you.

You will experience His kingdom on earth right here right now. Personal restoration and healing will come into your past relationships as you begin to understand the way the orphan spirit works. You will begin to see those who hurt you with Daddy's eyes.

The more you in live in intimacy with the Father the more you will release the Father's heart to others. You can begin encountering the Father right now.

Activation Prayer:

'Father, thank you that I am your son/daughter whom you love and in whom you're well pleased. Thank you that there is nothing that I can do that will separate me from your love. I love you, Daddy God. I choose to be led by the Spirit as your son/daughter today. Thank you that your love and your kingdom is already inside me. I lean into your heart more and more. I love you, Father'.

Immediately I hear Him say *'I love you too, son'*. *'I love you too, daughter'*.

'I ask you, Father, for release of more of the Father's heart'.

Take a minute or two to soak in His amazing love. Keep telling Him how much you love Him and listen for His response to you. Now love others with your Father's love.

Chapter 6

LIVING AS A CHILD OF THE FATHER

My father was what his generation called 'a man's man'. He grew up during the great depression of the 1920s and 30s and went to war as a teenager. Like many men of his generation, he believed that 'men do not show emotion or cry'. This was very difficult for me as a boy because I was regularly breaking bones, doing unusual things like burning my feet, jumping out of trees without realizing how hard the ground was, and crushing my hands in washing machine rollers. As a child I was often in the emergency room at the hospital where my father would always remind me that no matter how much I'd hurt myself, 'men don't cry.'

So it was not surprising that there was very little outward affection or any emotion ever shown by my father to my mother, my brothers and sister and me.

This type of upbringing later caused a problem for me when it came to relating to God as a loving Father. I did not have any idea how to do that. It came to a head one weekend when our church was having a series of revival meetings. We had asked some friends from another city to lead worship and minister in the power of the Holy Spirit that Saturday night. God's presence was growing as the night proceeded. When the worship leader began to say over and over, '*Daddy God loves you*' the presence of God invaded the room. It was glorious. I even felt the Father's presence even though I had such an orphan heart. Then the worship leader went further. He said, '*Now imagine Daddy God wrapping His arms around you and cradling you close to His chest like a father would a little child*'. My heart was being overcome with my Father's love.

But what he said next snapped me out of that encounter. He declared, '*Now your father is kissing you on your lips*'. I started to freak out. I had never experienced my earthly father kissing me like that, so how could I ever imagine my heavenly Father doing the same thing? I struggled for the rest the night and I knew I had a problem.

The reality was that I knew with my head that my heavenly Father loved me but I had never experienced it with my heart. I still lived with an orphan spirit – not as a son of God.

When you do have an actual encounter with the Father heart of God it changes you. Period! It especially changes the way you relate to God and others.

When we lived in Los Angeles during the early 1990s, we had a large family of five very young children. Even though

I was studying full time at seminary, I also had to work part time as we had very little income. We were struggling to make ends meet and had a poverty mentality that life was tough and we were poor. Something happened one day that helped change my perspective. I read an article in the Los Angeles Times about a man in Chicago who had been been homeless in winter and finally froze to death one night sleeping in his car. Even sadder was that he was the only surviving relative of a multi-millionaire uncle who had left all his inheritance to this man six months before. The uncle's lawyers had been trying unsuccessfully to find his nephew and tell him the good news of his multi-million dollar inheritance. All that time he was a wealthy man and did not have to be homeless. He just didn't know what belonged to him through His family inheritance. As I reflected on this again recently I realised that most people don't know that they also have an amazing family inheritance from their heavenly Father so they don't have to live as orphans. As soon as you realise that you are Daddy's sons and daughters you will change your outlook on life and the way you see others. Father God loves to bless His children. When you belong to God Father as a 'Christ one" or 'Christ-ian' (one is of Christ) you become the sons and daughters of God. His favor and blessing flows freely to His sons and daughters. You enter into His family. His life is infused into your life. Your Father's favor goes before you, and surrounds you and protects you. You begin to live in the blessing of your Father. You even change the way you relate to others.

Jesus says it best in John 5:20,

'For the Father loves the Son and shows him all he

does. Yes, and he will show him even greater works than these, so that you will be amazed'.

Not only does the Father show His son Jesus to you, He will also show His love through you to those around you.

As you step into the blessing of the Father, a realm of love is realised into you so you begin to transform all you relate to on a daily basis. He will impact others through you.

His love flowing in you will bless you. His love flowing through you to others will amaze others.

Before we go deeper into all the wonderful blessings and implications of the spirit of sonship –being Daddy God's sons and daughters, let's remember two crucial truths.

We Experience Intimacy with the Father

As we have seen in previous chapters, the most significant change is you are immediately ushered into a realm of intimacy with Him that you have not experienced previously;

He actually transforms your heart spiritually with the 'spirit of sonship.' There is such transformation that you even call out audibly 'Abba' or 'Father.'

Galatians 4:6 says it this way,

'Because you are his sons, God sent the Spirit of his Son into our hearts, the Spirit who calls out, 'Abba', Father.'

It is immediate because you instantly sense his overwhelming acceptance and limitless love.

Because it is intimate, you can hear His voice more clearly than you ever could previously. In my experience it was like God's still small voice was turned up to a normal speaking volume. You sense His amazing presence in your heart instantly even when you are not focusing on Him. When you tell Him that you love Him, you hearHim telling you in reply how much He loves you. It is a heart-to-heart connection that compares to nothing else you can ever experience. His deep limitless love instantly is revealed into your heart.

Your Identity Changes to Being His Child

Two remarkable things happened at Jesus' baptism. First, Jesus was baptized in the Holy Spirit,

Luke 3:21-22 says,

'When all the people were being baptized, Jesus was baptized too. And as he was praying, heaven was opened and the Holy Spirit descended on him in bodily form like a dove'.

Then the audible voice of God the Father was heard by all yes, yes were present. What did the Father say?

'You are my Son, whom I love; with you I am well pleased.'

We can only imagine how Jesus felt! He would have been so blessed to hear the Father say that about Him.

When you experience the sonship of the Father you become His beloved Son or daughter. So much so that as you read Luke 3:22 it is not presumptuous to superimpose your name in place of the son of God!!

Your sonship is that powerful! It is that real! It is that wonderful.

Why don't you declare it right now!

Activation Decree:

Declare this over yourself:
'I am His son/daughter ……..'
'I am His precious son/daughter…….'
'I am His precious son whom He loves….'
'I am His precious son with whom He is well pleased.'

As you decree that powerful revelation, I sense Him declaring over you...

'You are MY Son/Daughter…'
'You are MY Son/Daughter whom I love.'
'I AM pleased with you.'

Something wonderful happens inside you when you get this revelation. Deep in your heart you begin to truly believe that 'I am HIS son/ HIS daughter.'
Over and over again you hear him saying, 'I love you I love you I love you'.

Allow this to sink deeply into your soul!
Allow Him to reveal just who you have really become!
You are His son… His precious son.
You are His daughter… His precious daughter.
Declare it at loud *'I am HIS!'*
Not just any son/daughter, but His precious son/daughter!

Chapter 7

Your Inheritance as Daddy's child

If you're born into a family, you automatically become an heir to the family's legacy. The kingdom of God is no different: When you become adopted as a child of God, besides experiencing His intimacy and stepping into the fullness of your identity, you also gain an inheritance.

This is yet another benefit of intimacy with the Father – your inheritance. Paul understood the power of inheritance very clearly. In Galatians 4:7 he said,

> 'And since you are His child, God has also made you an heir.'

If you are an heir, then you have an inheritance. No one can take that from you!

What Does Your Inheritance Look Like?

'Now if we are children, then we are heirs—heirs of God and co-heirs with Christ...' – Romans 8:17a

It is one thing to be an heir, but what is a co-heir? It means to be a joint heir of a relative's estate. The term suggests that there is more than one of you but the good news is that you will all get an equal share of your Father's inheritance.

So what do you inherit with your co-heir Jesus Christ? Romans 8:17 continues,

'...if indeed we share in his sufferings in order that we may also share in his glory'.

This is incredible and stretching in many ways.

Share In His Suffering

In order to partake of His inheritance as sons and daughters, first we must be ready to share in His suffering. Before you get alarmed, let me explain.

There is a cost to receiving your inheritance. It is called not living for yourself! Paul explains it best:

'Do you not know that your bodies are temples of the Holy Spirit, who is in you, whom you have received from God? You are not your own; you were bought at a price. Therefore honor God with your bodies.'

– 1 Corinthians 6:19-20

I discovered one of the keys to how to respond when you realize that there is a cost in the kingdom of God – Just go ahead and pay it immediately. You just need to cross that bridge. So many Christians pull away from this experience because they believe that God is a 'good God' so they don't have a concept of suffering. But it is His goodness that leads us to tough things – like repentance. That is when He is truly treating us as sons and daughters.

'…not realizing that God's kindness is intended to lead you to repentance?' –Isaiah 65:1

'For whom the Lord loves He corrects, Just as a father the son in whom he delights.' – Proverbs 3:12 (NKJV)

Nothing is too much for God to ask because He has paid the ultimate price. His gave His Son to take our place so we ALL could be His sons and daughters. When you realize you are loved like that – you can love Him in return and pay any price that seems necessary.

The great news is that His grace is sufficient for you. You know that God's Word is true. So when He says there is nothing that you cannot handle – His grace makes a way for you!

Is it not much to ask for it to cost a little in return? In the process of your metamorphosis, which includes your cost and your suffering, you are being transformed more and more into His sonship!

So just settle it in your heart right now.

It is important to understand that you have to share in His suffering first before you can share in His glory. Like Jesus there has to be a dying to self.

As Jesus prayed in the garden (Matthew 26: 29),

'Not my will but your will be done.'

And as Paul prayed in Galatians 2:20,

'It is no longer I who live but Christ lives in me.' (NKJV)

You are a co-heir in Christ to share in His suffering so you can …

Share in His glory

Sharing His glory sounds better than sharing His suffering. But the truth is that you can't have one without the other.

Paul sums it up best in Romans 8:18,

I consider that our present sufferings are not worth comparing with the glory that will be revealed in us.

So once we cross the suffering bridge, we are blinded by the greatness of His glory. Once you have tasted of that glory, your suffering seems minute and barely noticeable.

His glory is not just a certain portion you receive once and for all. It is ever increasing!

2 Corinthians 3:18 tells us what happens when we begin to contemplate what His Glory is really like.

And we all, who with unveiled faces contemplate the Lord's glory, are being transformed into his image with ever-increasing glory, which comes from the Lord, who is the Spirit.

An instant metamorphosis takes place inside us. The word 'transformed' is only used twice in New Testament; here in 2 Corinthians 3:18 and also in Romans 12:2. Both times it means an ongoing supernatural transformation into God's image.

In other words, as God's heir, you not only *receive*, you *become!*

ACTIVATION DECREE:

'I am being transformed into His image'.

You experience that metamorphosis that transforms your DNA from being an orphan to a Son of God!

Your actual image changes into His image. Wow! That is when you truly experience 2 Corinthians 5:17:

"...the old has gone the new has come".

And if His glory is *'every increasing,'* then there is no measure or end to it! You can experience God's glory without limits!

That is why the early Apostolic fathers referred to it as 'ecstasy' or the 'ecstatic.' It is the realm of continuous, overflowing love of the Father with no limit to its depth or containment.

'For as high as the heavens are above the earth, so great is his love for those who fear him'. – Psalms 103:11-12

Activation Decrees:

'That's me!'
'I have the ever increasing transformational love of the Father working inside me.'

As Romans 8:39 says,

'Neither height nor depth, nor anything else in all creation, will be able to separate us from the love of God...'

Decree:

'The limitless ecstatic love of God the Father is transforming me in to His son/daughter.'

The world is waiting for you to get this.

In fact, the whole creation is waiting!

Chapter 8

THE REAL YOU IS BEING REVEALED

The more you begin to live out of your sonship, the more the real you becomes revealed!

It is wonderful when you see people being transformed into the fullness of their personality and identity–especially if they had a childhood that was inhibited by abuse, bullying or lack of opportunity. Once a transformed person begins to be revealed... look out!

Romans 8:19 says,

'Creation has been EAGERLY waiting for us to BE REVEALED as the CHILDREN of God'.

There was an old custom in Australia called 'Making your Debut'. The concept was originally from England. The word debutante is from the French word *débutante*, which means 'female beginner.' The debutante was a girl or young lady (normally sixteen to eighteen) who had reached the age of maturity and was introduced to society as an adult at a formal 'debut' ceremony. Originally, it meant the young woman was now eligible to marry, so part of the purpose was to display her to eligible bachelors and their families. In Australia debutantes may have been recommended by a committee or were sponsored by a member of a service club like the Lions or Rotary club. It was a big deal. It involved lots of preparation. Each girl was dressed in a special dress and formal hairstyle. Then they were presented to the community in which it was declared their time had come!

These events in Australia have now been replaced by high school senior formal events. But the concept is very powerful!

I hear the Lord saying,

'*I am revealing you like a young person to the world as My Son and My daughter!*'

'*It is your time. It is time for you to be revealed!*'

'*It is your first appearance, launch, or public introduction of being My SON – My DAUGHTER.*'

Activation Decree:

'It is time for me to be revealed as His Son/His Daughter!'

Creation Is Waiting For You to Be Revealed!
(Romans 8:19-22)

Being revealed is not to be taken lightly – In fact, all of creation is waiting for you to be revealed as a child of God.

It is time for you to come forth! You yes, yes revealed when you come into the fullness of your sonship.

'For the creation waits in eager expectation for the children of God to be revealed'. (v.19)

Verses 20-21 give us a picture of what it has been like for creation:

'For the creation was subjected to frustration, not by its own choice, but by the will of the one who subjected it in hope. For creation itself will be liberated from its bondage to decay and brought into the freedom and glory of the children of God.'

The New Living Translation expresses it this way:

'Against its will, all creation was subjected to God's curse. But with eager hope, the creation looks forward to the day when it will join God's children in glorious freedom from death and decay'.

Your sonship is so powerful that it even impacts how creation exists and functions. At the moment, all of creation has a life cycle. It is subject to decay. You see flowers bloom beautifully yet in a few days those same flowers begin to die.

Paul says it is in bondage to this decay and that it longs to be liberated and brought into freedom.

In v. 22 Paul likens this longing to it groaning for liberty. Paul says this is the same type of groaning that a woman experiences when she is in childbirth.

'For we know that all creation has been groaning as in the pains of childbirth right up to the present time'. (NLT)

You don't have to look far to see creation groaning – Whether it is a species of animals on the brink of extinction or a species of plant life that is no longer flourishing. While there are natural causes of decay in nature, many would argue that it is the result of human's actions that is causing most of this decay. Whether it is the illegal ivory hunters in Africa or the oil spills in fishing grounds, there is a distinct link to creation groaning and the greed of humankind acting like selfish orphans who can't get enough, no matter what the cost to others or to creation.

Your Body Is Waiting for Your Sonship to Be Revealed

Our bodies were never meant to deteriorate. We were meant originally to live for forever. When the seed of sin entered humanity we shifted from being sons of God to sons of man. At that time our bodies moved from eternal existence to finite existence When Jesus came to be a ransom sacrifice for us, our spiritual being or man was redeemed and reconciled to God. But our physical being still deteriorates and dies.

So there is still a groaning that is taking place with us. This is not a groaning of our joints as our bodies grow old. Romans 8:23 describes it as follows:

'Not only so, but we ourselves, who have the first fruits of the Spirit, groan inwardly as we wait eagerly for our adoption to sonship, the redemption of our bodies.'

Did you just get that? The more your spirit of sonship is revealed in you the more your bodies are actually redeemed.

You have the firstfruits of the spirit when you truly come into the revelation of being the Sons and Daughters of God.

So the more you live in intimacy with the Father and your identity as a son of God, the more you can step into your inheritance of living in more and more glory of God as a co-heir in Christ.

What would it be like if we were to actually step into what Moses experienced in Exodus 34:29-35?

He showed that it was possible step into a realm of glory where one's face shines and it seems the aging process is slowed down and even suspended. Yet our experience as sons and daughters is to be even better … whereas His glory began to fade away … ours is ever increasing! (see 2 Corinthians 3:13,18)

I would encourage you to explore even more what it means to have the redemption of our bodies as a co-heir of Christ that 'shares in His glory.'

You Were Always Intended for Sonship

Years ago I heard the story of a family in Australia who adopted a child from a war-ravaged nation that was also in the midst of famine. Each night as the family sat at the dinner table with their adopted child they began to notice after the meal the child was hiding something inside the front of his shirt. They discovered he was taking extra bread rolls to his room each night. He wasn't doing that because he was still hungry. He was hoarding food because he had lived so long as an orphan without enough to eat that he was frightened that the supply of food would end and he would be starving again.

Sadly, he didn't realize that now he was a son of a father and mother who would make sure that there would always be enough food. He was still groaning as an orphan even though he was now a son!

We must not let the same happen to us!

Paul says in Ephesians 1:3-4,

'Praise be to the God and Father of our Lord Jesus Christ, who has blessed us in the heavenly realms with every spiritual blessing in Christ. For he chose us in him before the creation of the world to be holy and blameless in his sight.'

He goes on to say in verse 5…..

'IN LOVE he predestined us for adoption to sonship through Jesus Christ, in accordance with his pleasure and will'.

There are two important truths for us here:

We are predestined for adoption to sonship. God predestined you to experience this amazing Father Heart of God. It was His plan from the beginning.

Ephesians 1 is not the only place you see this! In fact, it is amazing how many times the spirit of sonship is seen in the Bible.

Romans 8:29 also unpacks this with power! What is astounding is that the verse right before it, one of the most well known verses in the New Testament, is quoted completely out of context.

As Romans 8:28 says,

'And we know that in all things God works for the good …'

So often people say that without realizing that this is conditional. What does the Father want in return?

'….of those who love Him'

It is a promise for those who are sons and daughters of the Father...

'...who have been called according to his purpose'.

But you are not supposed to stop reading there!!

It goes on…

Romans 8:29 begins:

'For those God foreknew he also…'

What?

'...predestined.'

It is the same word as in Ephesians 1:5.

'He predestined us for adoption to sonship through Jesus Christ, in accordance with his pleasure and will.'

What was so important to God that He destined for all of human kind before any of us were even created? Let's keep on reading Romans 8:29.

'...to be conformed...'

To be conformed to what?

'...the image of his Son'.

This is God's ultimate plan for you!

God desired from the very beginning that all of humankind would be His sons and daughters! This was not an afterthought or an additional extra. This was in the heart of our Father before the foundation of the world.

We had our children in close succession. At one stage we had five children ages eight and younger. Every night I would read to them and pray for them as they lay in bed. Then after I turned the light out I would stand at their bedroom doors and sing worship songs to them until they went to sleep. Sometimes I would linger even after they had fallen asleep and watch them.

My heart would ache with love for my children.

As I began to pray into this I realized that it was because they were bone of my bone, flesh of my flesh. I would die for them in an instant. I wouldn't even have to think about it. My life for theirs! Done!

Why? They are mine and I am theirs! Yet, how much more does your Father love you? You are His sons and daughters.

However, we're not done with Romans 8:29 just yet. Let's keep reading…

> 'For those God foreknew he also predestined to be conformed to the image of his Son,) that he might be the firstborn among many brothers and sisters'.

All of us are predestined for this amazing experience to be His Sons/His Daughters. God doesn't play favorites, preferring some sons and daughters over others.

In this same spirit, our motivation must be to love our father, brothers and sisters no matter what!

There is more…

> And those he predestined, he also called; those he called, he also justified; those he justified, he also glorified. (v. 30)

Called to do what? To fulfill the call of God into your sonship. You have been predestined to always be part of His family, even before the beginning of the world.

ACTIVATION DECREE:

'I am called.
I can easily obey Him because I am loved without limits unconditionally.

I am justified in the place of being right with God every day
It is a new day every day for me.
It is a new era of knowing that He loves me as His Son/Daughter.

I am glorified.
I now know how to live in His glory.'

So when He says in Proverbs 29:11, 'I know the plans I have for you...' all you have to do is to do what He wants to please Him! As Paul says in Galatians 4:4 that the *set time* is now!

ACTIVATION DECREE:

'It is my set time as God's Son/Daughter'
Because I am His son / daughter, God has sent the spirit of His son into my heart, the spirit who calls out, 'Abba, Father.'

You have to step into it today together as His sons and daughters!

Chapter 9

SOARING IN YOUR SONSHIP ON PURPOSE

So many people do not live in freedom. Even Christians often live tied down to circumstances and to the orphan ways of seeing themselves and their lives.

The good news is that Jesus Christ broke the power of bondage to your old mindsets and lifestyles. You are no longer slaves to fear, intimidation, shame or control but rather you are sons and daughters of righteousness. You know you are able to live – even soar – in your freedom as sons of God, no longer allowing circumstances to rule over you. You now are able to soar in your life as you live for Him. His transformation is not only spiritual, it is practical.

The Father doesn't want you to just exist, He wants you to soar in the fullness of your sonship as His sons and daughters.

One of the main things God is saying to His sons and daughters is that that now is the time to soar!

Isaiah 40:31 says,

'But those who hope in the Lord will renew their strength. They will soar on wings like eagles; they will run and not grow weary, they will walk and not be faint'.

Recently I heard a friend teach on this verse. He was very intuitive and creative in how he taught it. Instead of beginning with soaring, he reasoned that when hope starts to increase you need to 'walk' before you can 'run.' He is right. There is no way you can run before you have learnt to walk. This also applies to how you live with God as your Father.

As the reality of His love and acceptance increases, we move from walking to running as a lifestyle. But there is one more step.

Papa God says, *'Son, daughter I don't just want you to run. I want you to soar. I want you to soar in my love'.*

To soar means you begin to truly see and live from your heavenly Father's perspective. When you soar, you are able to immediately change your way of seeing life when Papa God says, 'Come up here and see what I see.' This is a whole new way of living.

Paul refers to this as us ruling and reigning with Him:

And God raised us up with Christ and seated us with him in the heavenly realms in Christ Jesus.

– Ephesians 2:6

This is an important initial step as Daddy's child.

Your soaring needs to go up another level. The key to a soaring mindset is to live in the simplicity of God's love and see life with clarity through the Father's eyes. You can see the big picture when you are seated with Him in heavenly places.

New Era

There is a whole new emphasis on the Father's heart in this New Era. What does this big picture look like?

For a number of years now, we have been proclaiming it is a 'new season.' However, we realized that this new season seemed to be lasting a long time, so we began to ask '*How long does this new season last?*'

It was then that we realized it was not a new season. It is a whole new era!

By definition, an 'era' is *an 'extended period of time usually characterized by a distinctive development or by a memorable series of events.'*

We don't always see that it is a new era as it is unfolding. However, the more you soar in the Father's love, the more you see the bigger picture. This allows you to be more focused and even more intentional in your day by day life.

There has been so much change in society today. This change has accelerated significantly in the last few years. Yet, this change has not been reflected in the context of the church. Most leaders are beginning to understand that what worked previously in church life no longer works. A whole new operating system is needed in this new era. This is especially important when we begin to talk about the need for revival of the church and awakening of society.

Jesus warned in Mark 2:22 that when new wine is poured out, you need a new wineskin to contain it.

'And no one pours new wine into old wineskins. Otherwise, the wine will burst the skins, and both the wine and the wineskins will be ruined. No, they pour new wine into new wineskins'.

We need to change the way we see ourselves and others to allow the flow of the 'new wine' of the Father's love so we can soar in this new era.

How do you soar in this new era?

One of the joys of encountering the Father heart of God is that I am often asked by emerging leaders and emerging apostles if I would mentor them in this new era. I am always honored by these requests and I take them very seriously as each is an opportunity to potentially impact generations to come. It is important that we truly learn how to mentor or father with a next generation mindset. Regardless of how much time I can spend with these people, I try to cover three most important areas – Your Purpose, Your Position and Your Posture as Sons of God.

Your Purpose as Sons

Every son and daughter of God is born with a divine purpose. Therefore it is very important to know your purpose in life. I have discovered that most Christians either do not know their God-given purpose or they are not able to articulate that purpose out loud to others. They will say things like 'I just love the Lord' or 'I just want to worship God' or 'I just want to serve Jesus.' All these things happen more powerfully when you truly understand your unique God-given purpose. Success in life for a Christian is finding that unique purpose and doing it with your whole heart!

One of our friends is a successful middle-aged businessman. Recently he commented, *'I need to find me.'* What was he actually saying? In reality he was declaring, *'I need to find my God-given unique purpose and do it for the rest of my life.'*

This is a divine purpose that is uniquely yours. No other person has the same God purpose as you do. This is why you were created.

Psalms 139:16 says,

'Your eyes saw my unformed body; all the days ordained for me were written in your book before one of them came to be'.

Isn't that incredible? You are the only person who can fulfil God's plan for your life.

Jeremiah 29:11 says,

'For I know the plans I have for you,' declares the Lord, 'plans to prosper you and not to harm you, plans to give you hope and a future'.

This is the reason why you were created! Once you have found your unique God-given purpose, you need to jump into it.

Steve Harvey is an author, radio interviewer and television personality in the United States. Among other things he hosts the television show Family Feud. While he became infamous on social media because of a mistake he made announcing the Miss World beauty pageant winner in 2015, he did not allow that to define him. Why? Steve Harvey knows who he is and he knows his God-given purpose.

Something that is not well known about Steve Harvey is that he always speaks to his audience after the show is finished taping. Recently the cameras were inadvertently left on and he was unaware that what he was saying was being recorded.

As he addressed the audience, he said something very important. He was talking about the need for every person in life to define their God-given purpose for which they were created. He then declared *'Every person needs to JUMP.'*

There comes a time where you just need to step into that purpose. To do so, you need to jump! You need to do something to make it happen!

He went on to explain that every person is born with a

unique gift or destiny from God. But it does not just happen. You have to walk towards that destiny. When you take that step of faith, God makes room for you to take another step, then another and another.

When you do that, it creates an opportunity to grow into the next stage of your destiny.

'A man's gift makes room for him'. – Proverbs 18:16

Your God-given purpose makes room for you as you take a leap or even a step of faith.

Many years ago we had the honor of leading a church reaching out to 'street people' on the Gold Coast in Australia. One of the things that made it so unique was that we reached out to people in the street, parks and even jails using hip hop music and dance followed by testimonies by amazing young men and women who had been set free by Jesus from addictions of every kind.

One year we were asked to take our outreach team to Denpasar, Indonesia. The plane was delayed for over six hours. When we finally arrived, even though we were very tired we were asked to bring two of our team to be interviewed live on radio during a prime time talk back show. We agreed to go ahead with the interview. After a few questions it became very obvious that they were more interested in talking to the team members who had been set free from drug addictions rather than me. The interview was supposed to last twenty minutes but it lasted a lot longer. After listening for over 90 minutes in the studio I became so tired that

I fell asleep. Not only did I go to sleep, but I also snored live on national radio! Suddenly, I awoke to the interviewer and my team members looking at me with shocked looks on their faces. I whispered, *'Did my loud snoring just go live over the radio?'* They nodded in unison! I was horrified. Over three million people listening that night heard me snore live in the middle of an interview!

I can guarantee you that I was alert for the remainder of our time in the studio. As they wrapped up, I heard Father God say to me *'Son, most people sleep through their entire destiny.'* Sadly, this is all too true! Most people go through their entire lives oblivious to their God-given destiny. Even if they are aware of their destiny they spend so little time walking towards it. The truth is that you have to do more than that for your destiny to be fulfilled in your lives.

The secret to true happiness in life is finding God's destiny for your life and living it to the fullest. So many Christians act like their destiny will just 'happen' for them. It is as though they will wake up one day in the future and will be living in the fullness of their destiny, without having done anything for this to take place. This is not true. Your destiny doesn't just 'happen.'

You have to do something!

You need to find your unique destiny and JUMP into it.

So many people don't know how to do that. The easiest way is to be honest with yourself and ask, 'Who am I truly living for?'

When the answer to that question is 'God' then you are ready to answer the next destiny question.

What is your God-given passion?

Some may have problems articulating this passion, so this follow up question makes it significantly easier.

If you had unlimited opportunity, unlimited time, and unlimited money and resources what would you do for the glory of God?

I remember that when I was first asked this question, it was as if my God destiny was laid out in full detail before me.

Once you begin to see it, the best way to articulate this is to prayerfully write out what you hear and see.

If you are having some difficulty still answering the 'destiny question,' ask yourself another question, *'What am I good at?'*

Everyone is good at something! God made us that way. It can even be something very basic like mowing lawns. Steve Harvey tells the story of a man who realized that and decided to jump into a business of mowing lawns. Five years later he owned a multimillion-dollar lawn mowing franchise. Your destiny doesn't have to be business centered but it is wonderful when you are paid to do what you love to do.

If you still do not know what your God-given, unique purpose is in life and you would like to know more, my first book, *Fathering a Destiny - Growing Spiritual Sons and Daughters*, will help you explore this with greater depth than here.[1]

Paul was very clear in 2 Corinthians 13:5 where he says that we ought to be honest enough to examine ourselves. Examine how you are living and what you are doing with your life.

'Examine yourselves to see whether you are in faith......'

Another version says, 'Test yourselves.' (NASB).

Test what you're doing now! Does it fulfill you? Are you honestly living your God purpose?

Once you have discovered this one thing then have the faith to jump out of your current occupation and into your destiny purpose for the rest of your life! You then begin to live out the purpose of God for your life.

It's time to be honest with yourself regarding how you are living. If you are not living your God purpose – your divine destiny, then decide to find it or define it, then jump into it!

To soar you have to jump into God's purpose.

After jumping into your destiny with a leap of faith then it is time to run the race of faith. The New Testament speaks a lot about running the race of your life. Paul was very passionate about Christians learning how to finish their race well. It is not how you start but how you finish.

In Acts 20:24 he says,

'However, I consider my life worth nothing to me; **my only aim** is to **finish the race** and complete the task the Lord Jesus has given me—the task of testifying to the good news of God's grace'. (Bold added.)

Paul tells Timothy towards the end of his life,

'I have fought the good fight, **I have finished the race,** I have kept the faith'. (Bold added.)

To be able to run like this, you have to run like Paul says in Hebrews 12:1-2,

'Therefore, since we are surrounded by such a great cloud of witnesses, let us throw off everything that hinders and the sin that so easily entangles. And let us run with perseverance the race marked out for us, fixing our eyes on Jesus, the pioneer and perfecter of faith. For the joy set before him he endured the cross, scorning its shame, and sat down at the right hand of the throne of God'.

Notice Paul says that the only way we can run with perseverance is to 'throw off everything that hinders'.

What is hindering you? Be honest.

Be willing to not only recognize what these things are but also to change what is necessary in order to 'run with perseverance.' Once you start to run your race of life with perseverance then you can be confident that you will run a long life and finish well.

One of the greatest stories in the history of the Olympic Games took place in 1992 in Barcelona, Spain. A runner from England, Derek Redmon, was competing in the Semi-finals of the 400 meters race in the main stadium. Derek was the favorite to win the gold medal and had been undefeated leading up to and during the Olympics. He was winning his race comfortably when a tragedy happened. He collapsed on the track, tearing his hamstring in his left leg. All the other runners passed him as he lay on the track in agony. Instead of retiring from the race he got up and tried to run again. Over and over again he would fall, get up and hobble towards the finish line. The crowd rose to their feet and began to cheer for him. They had forgotten who had won the race. Their entire focus was now on Derek as he attempted to finish the race that he had started.

In 2 Timothy 4:7, Paul says,

'I have fought the good fight, I have finished the race'.

But Derek's story does not finish there. Something happened that caused this event to be recorded as a highlight in the history of the Olympic Games. As he was attempting to finish the race, someone ran from the crowd to join him. Derek turned to push him away, but when he realized who it was, he agreed. His father had seen his son struggling to finish the race. He couldn't bear it anymore so he ran to his son and put his arm around him and walked with him to the finish line. The whole stadium rose to their feet as one and began to shout and applaud as Derek finished his race leaning on his father.

What a wonderful picture and example to follow! You will always finish your race of life if you lean on God the Father. In fact, He will do even more than that. When you truly lean into His heart, He lifts you off the ground and begins to soar with you through life.

The key is to keep leaning into His heart. How do you do that?

Hebrews 12:2 tells us:

'... FIXing our eyes on Jesus…' (Upper case added.)

Once you have a heart encounter with Daddy God, He becomes the center of your focus every time you pray. It is no longer about you trying to get close to God but it's all about Him.

He fills you with His strength to live life! If you've been knocked down, the good news is that there is no 'used by' date on God's opportunity for you to encounter Him. Let Him help you up so you can stand and lean into His heart. Before long you will be running again. But this time, it will be you finishing the race together with Him.

This is what happens when you allow God the Father to be the center of your life.

We need to soar with a whole heart!

The heart of the church has been maligned for so long. Once a heart is out of alignment it gets out of rhythm with itself. When people have an irregular heartbeat, doctors will often install a pacemaker to help make the heart beat regularly again. To gain a healthy heart, a realignment is needed. This is also true for you to get into time with the heartbeat of heaven. Then you are positioned to learn to soar with a whole heart!

The truth is that you need a daily 'heart massage' with the Father's love to have a whole heart. You have to experience Him intimately every day.

Activation Decree:

'I choose to have a 'heart massage' with the Father's love today.'
'I welcome you to teach me how to soar in your love.'

How do you develop a Father's heart encounter lifestyle?

It is important to develop a heart lifestyle of intimacy IN His love. The main way for this to happen is to carve out time with Him. That time can be any time of the day. Look for a time when your day is quieter – for me that is at night time and early morning. But look for that time to be intimate. It is so worth it! Once you begin to do this His love for you is reinforced through many expressions of life.

One of the ways that best reinforces His love for you is by allowing Him to speak to you by reading His Word. Once you have the Father's love on your mind you see it everywhere – especially in His Word. The Word of God also washes you from the mindsets of the world so you begin to think and speak more and more in line with the way you were created.

ACTIVATION DECREE:

'I chose to spend time with you in intimacy today'

Just a take a moment right now and focus on the Father's love. Invite Him to show you how much He loves you.

Our Intimacy Overflows

Growing in intimacy with the Father overflows into all our relationships with others. We are not only to love others but also to mentor them in the Father's love. To truly soar in Daddy's love, I believe that you should have three levels of mentoring taking place in your life.

First, we are called to reproduce ourselves by pouring ourselves into those disciples younger in God than us. Then we need peer-to-peer mentoring – those on our level who are just as passionate for God.

As Proverbs 27:17 says,

'As iron sharpens iron, so one person sharpens another'.

Then we need fathers and mothers who are ahead of us who can pour into our lives to help lift us into a whole new level of the heart of the Father.

As the Father's heart begins to grow in you, the overflow is a soft heart towards God. A genuine maturity rises in you. You have dealt with selfish ambition and your own agendas. Life and ministry is no longer about you. It is only about Him and others. You have moved from your purpose to the Father's kingdom purpose that now overflows out of you. You truly then have the heart of the Father.

Activation Decree:

'I am willing to pour myself into others so I can help them experience the heart of the Father.'

Chapter 10

YOUR SONSHIP POSITION

One of the most exciting things that begins to happen when you begin to soar is that your position changes.

Soaring higher always involves a change of position. Sometimes it is intentional by the Father. It is like He sets you into position – it's your sonship position. It is also the overflow of leading a spirit-led life as a Son of God.

There is so much repositioning going on right now in the body of Christ. Some of you have even experienced geographical repositioning. If you have ever watched an eagle soar you see they are willing to push up higher and higher. They know the higher they go the more clearly they see and the clearer the atmosphere and the easier it is to soar.

The more you soar, the more you change position and are repositioning for a higher purpose.

But the Father does not want this repositioning to happen through striving. You can't make soaring happen – He has to lift you into your God-intended position.

For example, I am often asked by younger leaders, *'How do you get an international ministry?'* because they desire to have one. My answer is always the same – God! The Father is the only one who can set you into that divine position.

Daddy God lifts you into that position when you have repositioned your heart and mindset so it is no longer about you, but Him! When He knows He has your heart, He is able to trust you with the hearts of others. This repositioning is often gradual and requires faithfulness on each new level. We learnt this many years ago from a wonderful prophet of God, Dick Mills, who really fathered us while he was briefly visiting our city. I have never forgotten what He said. He decreed Acts 1:8 over Cheryl and me and said that we would have an expanding sphere of influence – first in our town or city (our Jerusalem), then our region (our Judea), our state (our Samaria) and then the ends of the earth. That is exactly what has happened. It was one new position at a time.

Here are a few things that I have learnt that will help you in your current position:

Actively POSITION yourself into alignment with those who have the same DNA or same heart as you. One of the reasons there has been such an emergence of apostolic networks is that many sons and daughters have been discovering this and positioning themselves in apostolic alignment with spiritual fathers and mothers.

Actively REALIGN your thinking with the Word and will of God. Sometimes this will mean changing your normal operating system. It may even mean unlearning some of the ways you have been taught to do ministry. As one of my good friends in Africa says, 'We don't need our own culture, we need His kingdom culture'.

To do this, you must consciously allow God to SHIFT your perceptions and ways of doing ministry and even life.

Activation Decree:

'I choose to actively position myself today in you, Father.'
'I choose to realign my thinking with the Word and will of God.'

Daily Positioning Supernaturally

Being positioned supernaturally begins with learning to live in God's will for you each day.

As a son or daughter of God, you begin by accepting Paul's challenge in 1 Thessalonians 5:16-18 regarding how to live:

Rejoice always, pray continually, give thanks in all circumstances; for this is God's will for you in Christ Jesus.

There is power in learning how to rejoice, giving thanks in all circumstances (and not just the ones we enjoy), and learning how to pray continuously. This is how we learn to be led by the Spirit of God after we have received the spirit of adoption.

The next step is that you need to have the mind of Christ. It is no surprise that your mind needs to be renewed as you will soon discover you will still think like an orphan on a regular basis. In fact, I often catch myself reverting to old orphan thinking.

Romans 12:2 must become your mandate:

'Do not conform to the pattern of this world, but be transformed by the renewing of your mind. Then you will be able to test and approve what God's will is—his good, pleasing and perfect will'.

To truly soar you need to make sure you wash your brains daily. Yes! You need to be brainwashed in the blood of Jesus and the Word of God. So the Word of God becomes flesh IN us.

Paul teaches us how to do this in Colossians 3:2,

'Set your minds on things above, not on earthly things'.

In other words, you have to learn to soar with your thinking before you can soar in the Spirit. He goes on to teach how you can put off the flesh and put on Christ.

Paul says in Colossians 3:12-13 for us to:

'...as God's chosen people, holy and dearly loved, clothe yourselves with compassion, kindness, humility, gentleness and patience. Bear with each other and forgive one another if any of you has a grievance against someone. Forgive as the Lord forgave you.

He continues in verse 14...

'And over all these virtues put on love, which binds them all together in perfect unity'.

When you do this your thinking changes and your spirit man begins to rise over your natural way of responding to life challenges.

In the process you learn the rhythms of God's way of living. You learn to recognize the ways of God and you choose to live that way! I call this intentional positioning in the lifestyle of the Father.

Activation Decree:

'Father, teach me to get into step with the rhythms of your way of living'.
'I choose to learn how to recognize the ways of God and choose to live that way!'

Intentional Positioning

You need intentional positioning into where you need to live every day. As you have already learnt, unless you have intimacy with the Father, you will have nothing to stand on when your identity and authority are attacked.

Jesus had His identity and authority repeatedly challenged by religious leaders.

First in Matthew 16:1 He was asked to show them a *'miraculous sign.'* But we learn that was not enough for them. They didn't want to believe He was the son of God. That is why their questioned progressed to the next level in Mark 11:28 where He was confronted by the question *'By what authority'* was He doing those miracles? They were never going to be satisfied with what He answered because they had a mindset of unbelief.

Unbelief and offence go hand in hand. So it wasn't long that they were scornfully criticizing and mocking in Matthew 13:55, *'Isn't this the carpenter's son?'*

In other words, 'How could a carpenter's son be the king of the Jews that we have been waiting for?'

With that they dismissed the identity and authority of the Son of God and missed the miracle of ever becoming sons of God themselves.

One of things God has told us to do is to pour ourselves into emerging fathers and mothers in God. Why? Because this is what true spiritual fathers and mothers do. They help make a way for young fathers and mothers to emerge. For us to truly soar we need to have a next generation mindset.

To truly help others to soar, you need to be aligned with apostolic and prophetic fathers and mothers. When you understand this, you truly understand intentional positioning. I have learnt that you can pull on the authority through your identity as a son or daughter in that alignment.

When you know your position, you also know how to use your authority. One of the keys is through decrees.

In Job 22:28 you learn that there is power in your decrees. God said through Job, 'Decree a thing and it WILL be established'.

ACTIVATION DECREE:

'I position myself today through my decrees'.

Decrees work when they are used properly and consistently. The best decree resources that will help you learn to decree with authority is a compilation of decrees from God's Word.

Here is an example from Patricia King's book, *Decree a thing, and it shall be established.*[1]

'In Christ Jesus, I am favored by my heavenly Father. The favor He has given His Son has been given to me. It is undeserved, unmerited favor that is granted me in Christ. His favor is a free gift to me, for which I am very thankful. As Jesus kept increasing in wisdom and stature, and in favor with God and men, so also do I, because I abide in Jesus and He abides in me.'

I recommend that you get a copy of *Decree a thing, and It Shall Be Established* and use it to begin a lifestyle of decrees.

Chapter 11

Your Posture as a Son of God

Have you ever seen a person with a regal posture? They carry themselves differently from everyone else. You often hear people comment that certain persons have such a regal way about them, whether they are from a royal heritage or not. When they walk into a room people notice them. It is because of their posture.

There is also a posture that a son of God develops. When you grow into the fullness of your sonship, you carry yourself differently. Why? Because you know who your Father is and that you are His Son or daughter. You act like a son of God.

When you begin to intentionally position yourself in His sonship, there comes a change in your posture. Your posture changes as you soar into the heights of the Father's love. You begin to live your life from a completely different perspective. I have found that you become a lot more relaxed about things when they go wrong. You begin to see life and your circumstances through a posture of confidence as your Father is in charge and He will make a way.

When I was young, my mom was always concerned about me having the right posture. If I was standing in a slouched position she would walk up behind me and put her finger in my back and say, 'Bruce, stand up straight.' She knew that the way I stood then would govern the way I stood when I was older and I needed the right posture!

What Is the Posture of a Son?

I have learnt that the Father develops faith, authority and presence in our posture as Sons of God.

Faith Posture

When you have a posture of a Son, not only do you believe, you receive what God has for you. You are able to soar in faith in every situation. You grow a faith posture.

In Matthew 21, Jesus curses a fig tree. The disciples are amazed the next day when they see that the tree has died overnight.

They ask in Matthew 21:20,

'How did the fig tree wither so quickly?'

Jesus then teaches the powerful principle of a faith posture:

> 'Truly I tell you, if you have faith and do not doubt, not only can you do what was done to the fig tree, but also you can say to this mountain, "Go, throw yourself into the sea," and it will be done'.

When you truly understand the power of your faith posture, then your words are weighty with authority.

'If you believe, you will receive.'

This faith posture causes you to live in faith as a lifestyle. I have found that a faith posture moves you from having to exercise your faith to expectation of His blessing for your marriage, family, health, wealth and ministry before you have any need.

You will learn to live in the Shalom of God – nothing missing, nothing broken – and perfect in every way. This is your Faith Posture. So when you learn to live in favor, breakthrough and blessing; nothing throws you out of faith.

ACTIVATION DECREE:

Thank you that you are changing my posture into a Faith Posture.
Father, grow your faith posture in me.

Authority Posture

As the Son of God, Jesus spoke as 'one who had' great authority. That was one of the things that those who listened to Him for the first time noticed about Him. And it amazed them.

Luke 4:32,

'They were amazed at his teaching, because his words had authority'.

It wasn't just His teaching that had authority. He also had authority in the spirit realm.

Luke 4:36,

'All the people were amazed and said to each other, 'What words these are! With authority and power He gives orders to impure spirits and they come out!'

Jesus knew how to deal with the unexpected! Why? He had the authority posture of the Son of God!

This was evident in Matthew 8:28-30 when Jesus restored two demon-possessed men in Gaderenes. As soon as they saw Him, they sensed His authority and who He was and cried out,

'What do you want with us, Son of God?' they shouted. "Have you come here to torture us before the appointed time?"'

The result?

'He said to them, "Go!" So they came out and went into the pigs, and the whole herd rushed down the steep bank into the lake and died in the water. Those tending the pigs ran off, went into the town and reported all this, including what had happened to the demon-possessed men'. (v. 32-33)

People were afraid of the supernatural authority and they are still afraid today.

'Then the whole town went out to meet Jesus'. (v. 34a)

You would have thought they would have embraced Him and all become believers. No. We also learn that,

'When they saw him, they pleaded with him to leave their region'. (v. 34b)

I often find the same response today from some people who are even intimidated by the title of my book *Encountering the Supernatural*. [1]

They are afraid of anything that is not logical or natural – even some Christians respond this way. But the Christian life is supernatural. It has to be. It is the only way you can be born again, have your prayers answered through faith and be adopted as a son or daughter of God.

You also should have an authority posture as a son/daughter of God.

Jesus has given you and all believers authority over your circumstances, sickness and demons. This is what He taught His disciples in Luke 9-10.

How much more authority do you have as His son or

daughter? You have the keys to the kingdom of heaven as His Son and daughter. So when Jesus told Peter in Matthew 16:19, 'I will give you the keys of the kingdom of heaven; whatever you bind on earth will be bound in heaven, and whatever you loose on earth will be loosed in heaven', Jesus was also telling him he had the power to bind and loose here on earth and heaven. You have this same authority as well.

When you truly know who is in inside you, you step into your authority posture. When you adopt your authority posture you are able to let Him out!

I marvel at the response I receive from people when I share the flight to Mali mid air emergency flight story. Many people are stunned that I boldly preached the gospel.

But I didn't have to stop and think about what I should do in the midst of the possible crash of our aircraft. My boldness and actions just came out of my authority posture. And the circumstances responded accordingly and the plane was saved.

When you have an authority posture, it just overflows out of you.

Activation Decree:

'I choose to have an authority posture as His Son/Daughter.'

'I decree I have authority over circumstances in my life not in line with God's will for me.'

'As Daddy's son/daughter, I decree that ALL things out of order must come into alignment NOW with the Father's will in Jesus' name.'

Presence Posture

As well as your authority posture, you need a presence posture. Have you ever experienced the spiritual atmosphere change when someone has walked into a room? I've personally experienced that happen many times when people like Heidi Baker and David Hogan have entered into a church service midway through the meeting. You actually feel the atmosphere change. They have a presence posture.

The reason why they have a presence posture is that they spend so much time in the presence of God. But this posture is not just limited to a special few holy people. As a son/daughter of Father God, you also carry the same presence of His love wherever you go. This will become more and more evident when you have a presence posture.

You may ask, 'Are you sure that is possible?' Absolutely. This is the outcome of living a Spirit-controlled and Spirit-led life as a son and daughter of God.

Why is this so important? You represent your Father, so you need to carry Him wherever you go. When you have a presence posture you are able to bring the supernatural presence of God into every circumstance you walk into.

Paul had a presence posture. This is evidenced with His statement in 1 Corinthians 2:4 – 5,

> 'My message and my preaching were not with wise and persuasive words, but with a demonstration of the Spirit's power, so that your faith might not rest on human wisdom, but on God's power'.

In Romans 8, Paul taught us that as the spirit of sonship came from intimacy with Father, when you truly experience His adoption you begin to listen for and be led by the Spirit of the Father each day. It becomes a lifestyle of living in the presence of God.

The key is to always be looking to be Spirit-led. Listen for the Holy Spirit's leading in every part of your life. Look for His presence and consciously carry Him wherever you go.

Decide to soar in His presence. When you soar you get elevation and you see how the demonstration of the Holy Spirit's power is possible to move through you. Then the love of the Father will over flow out of you. You won't be looking for revival. It will be overflowing out of you.

You will shift atmospheres and live with a Presence Posture.

ACTIVATION DECREE:

'I choose to have a Presence Posture of the Father's love'.

'I step into the Spirit right now and sense His presence with me'.

'As I am led by the Spirit of God today, my sonship grows in me and the Father's heart flows out of me to others'.

His Purpose, His Position and His Posture are so important and so powerful. They cause you to 'soar' in the Father's love.

Just recently I was explaining these principles to one of my friends in the context of a very challenging family business situation. He shared the original vision of why he first began the business. He explained that it was to build the kingdom of God through his family for generations to come. The goal was that his business enterprises would have a Godly legacy through his children well after he was gone. His problem was that his adult son, who was working with him on a management level, was not walking with God and shared no interest in his father's Godly vision for the family company. So after we discussed the need to have a faith posture, authority posture and presence posture, he rose up and stepped into his new posture in God. He began to decree a shift in the transition of the company so it would maintain its Godly legacy.

A miraculous shift happened. Early the next morning, I received a message from my friend to say that his son had contacted him early that day to ask if he could meet with his father to discuss and pray about the future of the company. This had never happened before in all the years that they had been working together! Because of the meeting, his son caught the vision and came into unity with his father concerning the God vision for the future of the company.

This posture of living as a son of God works!

ACTIVATION DECREE:

'I choose to reposition myself with the Father's passion, position and posture.'

'I choose to soar today in my passion, positioning and posture.'

This is how you soar as a Son of God!

Conclusion

Congratulations. If you have begun to put into practice what you have read in this book, *The Father's Love,* you have stepped into the most exciting way to live in intimacy with the Father.

In fact, this is the way you were always meant to live. You have truly entered into the fullness of why you were created.

Praise God! You have truly become Daddy's Son/Daughter!

Now you are on this amazing journey for the rest of your life, becoming more and more like your Father every day as you are led by His Spirit.

The key to this ongoing transformation is encountering His Father heart daily. Allow God the Father to continually break into your life with His Spirit of sonship. As He wraps His arms of love around you and declares, 'I love you my Son,' 'I love you my daughter,' everything changes! Everything in your world comes into perspective and you begin to see with Daddy's eyes and soar in the power of His Holy Spirit.

You have begun a wonderful process. You are now living like a 'son of God'. The more you recognize the symptoms of an orphan heart in you, the more you will be able to invite the Father to heal whatever caused you to act that way. He then replaces it with the 'love of the Father' motivation. As you do, you will move from living like an orphan to becoming a true Son of God.

I hear Him declaring over you today, 'You are my son/my daughter in whom I am well pleased!'

He is so proud of you.

My prayer is that through reading this book you come to the place of experiencing the Father's love like never before.

You can use 'The Father's Love' daily as a workbook. Keep using the Activation Decrees. Pursue the Father and His love like never before.

Here are some final decrees that I hear from the heart of the Father for you.

Father Heart Decrees for you

He is saying:

'Receive even more of my love right now. Let my love overflow in you'

'Let there be a greater manifestation of the Father heart of God in you in Jesus' name.'

'Your Father God loves you. He loves you. He loves you.'

He is wrapping His arms around you right now and holding you close to His heart.

'He declares over you,

'You are my beloved son/daughter whom I love, in whom I am well pleased'.

He is pleased with you.

There is nothing you'll ever do that will separate you from His love.

Endnotes

Chapter 1- Why We Need the Father's Love

[1]Restore the Foundations Ministry
Restoring the Foundations
2849 Laurel Park Highway
Hendersonville, NC 28739
www.rtfi.org

Chapter 2- Becoming Sons and Daughters

[1]*How to experience the miracle of eternal life*

To become a true believer in Jesus Christ and experience eternal life is not hard at all. It just requires you to be honest with yourself and honest with God and to humbly ask Him to take control of your life from now on. If you have never done that before here is a simple prayer that you can use that will help you do just that:

ADMIT – *'Jesus, I admit that I need you. I cannot save myself and I need a saviour. I realise that my life has been self-centered and today I want to have you as the centre of my life '.*

Romans 3:23 puts it this way:
'All have sinned an fall short of the glory of God'
It is important to realise that you will never be good enough to save yourself. That is why you need a saviour! But there is another important fact here. The glory of God is your way into the supernatural. So to begin your supernatural journey you need to regain the distance that you have fallen short. Jesus is the only way to do that. Ask Him now.

ASK – *'I ask that you forgive me for my all sins (pause a moment here and be specific). Thank you for dying for me and taking the consequence of my sin. I ask that you come into my life and take control. I ask that you reveal your love to me.'*

God's Word declares this over you today in 1 John 1:9,

'If we confess our sins, he is faithful and just and will forgive us our sins and purify us from all unrighteousness.'

ACCEPT – *'I accept your free gift of love, forgiveness, acceptance and eternal life. I was blind but now I see. I accept you as my personal Lord and Saviour from today forward in Jesus name!'*

Congratulations. Welcome to the family of God! You are now a Christian – a Christ one!

So now you can step into the lifestyle of transformation. You get to live what you just began!

Chapter 9 - Soaring in Your Sonship on Purpose

[1] *Fathering a Destiny – Growing Spiritual Sons and Daughters* by Bruce Lindley
Australian Apostolic Restore Community (A.A.R.C.)
PO Box 4393, Helensvale B.C. QLD 4212 Australia
www.australianarc.org.au

Chapter 10 - Your Sonship Position

[1] *Decree:* Third Edition by Patricia King
XP Publishing P.O. Box 1017
Maricopa, Arizona 85139 USA
www.xpministries.com

Chapter 11 - Your Posture as a Son of God

[1] *Encountering the Supernatural* by Bruce Lindley
Australian Apostolic Restore Community (A.A.R.C.)
PO Box 4393, Helensvale B.C. QLD 4212 Australia
www.australianarc.org.au

Apostolic Resource Community International

(A.R.C. International)

Apostolic Resource Community International (A.R.C. International) incorporates Australian Apostolic Restore Community (A.A.R.C)

A.R.C. International is an international apostolic community of emerging apostles and prophets that exists to build the kingdom of God by walking together in strategic relationships, establishing Fire Houses of Prayer around the Pacific Rim nations and beyond, sending out Apostolic & Prophetic teams to Australia & the nations, and equip the body of Christ for revival!

A.R.C International is based in Australia and holds regular supernatural encounter events and also hosts international revival ministries in Australia.

A.R.C. International commissions emerging apostles and prophets and sets people apart in their gifts to do the work of the ministry

A.R.C. is apostolically aligned with Harvest International Ministries (H.I.M.), a world wide apostolic network.

Go to www.australianarc.org.au/About us for more information

Bruce Lindley's Other Books

Fathering a Destiny -
Growing Spiritual Sons and Daughters

A leadership book on the apostolic fathering reformation that will give you a next generation mindset and help you discover your God destiny and grow the destiny of others. You will learn how to position in your destiny.

Encountering the Supernatural

Encountering the Supernatural will take you on a journey to learn how to live in the supernatural on a daily basis and you will learn how to build an atmosphere of the supernatural. The supernatural truths that took our spiritual fathers generations to discover are available to you today!

Get ready to encounter a whole new realm of the supernatural

The Seeing Transformation

The Seeing Transformation reveals how God has always intended you to see life and your self and others. You will learn to live in the realm of remarkable miracles by changing the way you see! SEE your life transformed?

Then get ready to SEE like you have not seen before!

To Order

www.australianarc.org.au then go to the Resource page

To contact the Bruce Lindley to arrange speaking engagements or additional resources:

Email – admin@australianarc.org.au

www.ingramcontent.com/pod-product-compliance
Lightning Source LLC
Chambersburg PA
CBHW070622300426
44113CB00010B/1627